Celebrate His Coming

An Advent Devotional

JAYE BROWN

Inspirational. Positive. Encouraging.

CELEBRATE HIS COMING
By Jaye Brown
Published by TouchPoint Faith
An imprint of TouchPoint Press
www.touchpointpress.com

Copyright © 2017 Jaye Brown
All rights reserved.

ISBN-10: 1-946920-28-2
ISBN-13: 978-1-946920-28-7

No part of this book may be reproduced in any manner without the express written consent of the publisher, except in the case of brief excerpts in critical reviews or articles. All review copy and media inquiries should be addressed to media@touchpointpress.com.

TouchPoint Press books may be purchased in bulk or at special discounts for sales promotions, gifts, fund-raising, or educational purposes. For details, contact the Sales and Distribution Staff: info@touchpointpress.com or via fax: 870-200-6702.

Editor: Ashley Carlson
Cover Design: Colbie Myles, colbiemyles.com

Scripture taken from the HOLY BIBLE, NEW INTERNATIONAL VERSION®. Copyright © 1973, 1978, 1984 by International Bible Society. Used by permission of Zondervan. All rights reserved.

First Edition

Printed in the United States of America.

Dedication: Thank You, Jesus, for coming!

Contents

THE ADVENT SEASON	1
THE FIRST HALF — WHY JESUS CAME	3
December 1	5
Perhaps He's Not What We Expect	6
December 2	10
Perhaps He's Not What We Want	11
December 3	15
Let's Get a Couple Things Straight	16
December 4	20
We Have History Together	21
December 5	25
Bad Beginnings but Good Endings	26
December 6	30
A Line Across Christmas	31
December 7	35
Mission Possible	36
December 8	40
Someone Is After Us	41
December 9	45
Can You See Him Now?	46
December 10	50
Neither Half Empty Nor Half Full	51
December 11	55
Climbing the Ladder Downward	56
December 12	60
What Time Is It?	61
December 13	65
Plug in the Lights	66
December 14	70
Some Things Aren't Up for Discussion or Negotiation	71
THE SECOND HALF—HOW JESUS CAME	75
December 15	77
Someone Keeps Promises	78
December 16	82
Check Out These Credentials	83
December 17	87
Is It Really Him?	88
December 18	92

Let the Miracles Begin	93
December 19	97
Let the Grace Begin	98
December 20	102
Bolstering Belief	103
December 21	107
Let the Rejoicing Begin	108
December 22	112
There's Been a Change of Plans	113
December 23	117
What Exactly Just Happened?	118
December 24	122
Look Who Received an Invitation	123
December 25	127
Check the Gift Tag	128
December 26	132
One Step at a Time	133
December 27	137
Being in the Know	138
December 28	142
Look Who Else Was Invited	143
December 29	147
You're Not the Boss of Me	148
December 30	152
Sin, Sorrow, and Salvation	153
December 31	157
The Plan Prevails	158

The Advent Season

The English word "advent" is derived from the old Latin word "adventus," meaning "arrival." Historically, it designated the arrival of someone or something notable. Among Christians, the word is used to refer to the coming of Jesus as a baby in Bethlehem. For churches that follow a liturgical year, Advent is the first season of the church calendar, but it has been popularized beyond this formal role to be the time during which all Christians prepare their hearts for Christmas.

To be precise, Advent begins four Sundays before Christmas Day and ends on Christmas Eve. Both in sanctuaries and in homes, the weekly lighting of an Advent wreath's candles provides the opportunity to consider various aspects of Jesus' coming. The more widespread the celebration of Advent has become, the more variety there has been in wreaths and other practices. Candle colors might be any mix of purple, pink, and white, with various meanings assigned to each color. Sometimes a fifth candle is added to the center of the wreath for Christmas Day, extending the season beyond its formal duration.

In addition to the recitations that typically accompany the four-Sunday lighting of one or more candles, Advent devotionals provide daily readings and reflections in an effort to make the season even more substantive and meaningful. However, preparing such a devotional faces the challenge of the season itself changing in length from year to year along with the placement of the four Sundays, depending upon where December 25th falls in the week. Thus, the Advent season ranges from 22 to 28 days (not counting Christmas Day) and can start as early as November 27th or as late as December 3rd.

Following the spirit of a less rigid approach to celebrating Advent and wanting to accommodate any and all yearly calendars, this devotional offers daily meditations dating from December 1st through the 31st. Because this liberty is being taken, perhaps it should be called a Christmas devotional; yet there's something special about the ancient word Advent. It serves as a constant reminder that the season celebrates an arrival, a coming—the most notable one the world has ever known.

The First Half — Why Jesus Came

There are countless writings about why Jesus came to earth, from evangelistic pamphlets to scholarly commentaries. However, who better to provide the reasons than Jesus Himself? On several occasions throughout His earthly ministry, Jesus specified why He was sent and why He came. The first portion of this devotional invites the reader to spend each day pondering one of the reasons identified by Him for His coming. Some of them are familiar and thrilling, others are rarely quoted and can be perplexing or troubling, but each one comes from Jesus' heart to our hearts.

The trendy expression "Jesus is the Reason for the Season" reminds us to untangle Christmas from its commercial trappings enough to realize it is first and foremost a celebration of Jesus. The point being, if we busy ourselves with everything except the holiday's primary focus, then we've missed its meaning entirely. Similarly, Jesus' reason-for-coming statements indicate very precisely what His coming was intended to accomplish. If we fail to let Him accomplish these specific intentions in our lives, then we've missed the whole point of His arrival, <u>His</u> whole point.

December 1

For God so loved the world that he gave his one and only Son, that whoever believes in him shall not perish but have eternal life. For God did not send his Son into the world to condemn the world, but to save the world through him.

John 3:16-17 (from John 3:1-21)

Perhaps He's Not What We Expect

In addition to John 3:16 being one of the most familiar verses in all of Scripture, something else attests to its significance. If the four Gospels were arranged into one sequential account so that Jesus' mission statements appear in chronological order, John 3:16 would contain His first announcement of why He came. Whatever the other reasons, it's essential for us to embrace this reason.

However, despite its importance, it wasn't the reason many people expected. And, still today, it's not the reason many people expect.

The Jewish establishment in the first century certainly anticipated a Messiah but expected (and preferred) Him to come for different reasons than Jesus announced. For hundreds of years, the Old Testament promised His arrival. When He finally came, these religious people expected Him to affirm and elevate their "rightness," thereby, affirming and elevating them.

Instead, Jesus told one of them, a man named Nicodemus (v. 1), that it was necessary for him to be born again to see the kingdom of God (v. 3). This meant none of Nicodemus' right thinking or right living made him "right enough" with God. Even his recognition that Jesus was "from God" (v. 2) wasn't enough. Imagine someone so religious being told he was still lacking.

It's no wonder Nicodemus was surprised (v. 7). Jesus came to accomplish the opposite of what religious people often expect. Jesus, not Nicodemus, must be elevated (v. 14) as the sole provider of rightness with God. Jesus, not Nicodemus, is the One Nicodemus must believe in to receive new, eternal life (v. 15).

Stripped of their self-righteous status, religious people become no more advantaged than nonreligious people. This doesn't resolve the matter of expectations, though, because nonreligious people, despite their willingness to admit spiritual deficiencies, are just as likely to expect the wrong thing of Jesus. Perhaps because what they need seems mysterious (v. 8) or impossible (v. 4), they tend to expect Jesus to come with condemnation for their sins. This expectation is the reason so many people never darken the door of a church—if Jesus is inside, then they assume condemnation must be inside also.

However, Jesus' announcement of why He came proclaims just the opposite. His coming was wholly love-driven, not condemnation-driven (v. 16-17). Despite the fact that sinfulness deserves condemnation, Jesus was sent by God the Father to provide sin's remedy, its only remedy (v. 18). He was sent to provide the remedy that's needed by both religious and nonreligious people.

There's one other misconception that Jesus' announcement corrects. Because God the Father loves the whole world, Jesus was sent for the whole world. He would spend the rest of His earthly ministry identifying just how far-reaching and all-inclusive His coming was meant to be. On this occasion, it included someone so uncertain or hesitant or fearful that he approached Jesus by night rather than by the light of day (v. 2).

For such individuals, Jesus clarifies that the light that matters is the light He brings onto the scene (v. 19). Yes, it exposes a person's sins because it's the light of truth (v. 20), but it also makes something clear to everyone: what is accomplished by Jesus in our lives is the work of God (v. 21). He alone can exchange the self-credit of a religious person or the self-condemnation of a nonreligious person for new, eternal life.

Jesus' reason for coming may not be what everyone expects, but it's what everyone needs.

Prayer: I celebrate the coming of the One who enters our world and our lives with God's love. Whether I tend toward self-credit or self-condemnation, I put my trust in the righteousness provided by a loving God rather than my own righteousness. I welcome God's presence, love, and righteousness into my life this Advent season.

Notes:

Personal Prayer:

December 2

The Spirit of the Lord is on me, because he has anointed me to preach good news to the poor. He has sent me to proclaim freedom for the prisoners and recovery of sight for the blind, to release the oppressed, to proclaim the year of the Lord's favor.

Luke 4:18-19 (from Luke 4:14-30)

Perhaps He's Not What We Want

Jesus' earthly ministry was well underway when He made this formal declaration of His intentions. He had already performed at least one miracle (John 2), had explained the necessity of being born again (John 3), and had identified Himself as the Messiah (John 4). With God's Spirit resting mightily upon Him, "news about him spread through the whole countryside" of Galilee (v. 14), the northernmost province of Palestine, and "everyone praised him" (v. 15).

Then Jesus traveled to His hometown of Nazareth (v. 16) inside Galilee. This was where Joseph and Mary resided before His birth (Luke 2:4) and returned for His upbringing (Matthew 2:19-23; Luke 2:39-40). Unlike His birthplace of Bethlehem, which was small but steeped in Old Testament significance, Nazareth wasn't viewed as having the capacity to produce much of anything (John 1:44-46).

Perhaps hometown pride played a part in the people's welcome of Jesus. He was given the honor of reading Scripture during the synagogue service (v. 16-17). Whether He selected the Isaiah 61 material or it was assigned by the attendant, Jesus' pronouncement that the words were being fulfilled in their midst thrilled the crowd (v. 20-22). They knew these words described the Messiah, the One eagerly awaited by all of Israel for centuries. This remarkable prodigy from their own dusty village announced His arrival as well as His mission.

And, what a mission it was! Whether the description of His target audience (v. 18) was to be understood literally or figuratively, it was clear that this Mighty One would help the lowly and needy. For Him to be marked by such grace was cause for amazement (v. 22). Best of all, He was theirs (v. 22); so they anticipated miracles in their midst (v. 23).

Then, suddenly, everything changed. Their excitement and receptivity turned to anger and hostility, even an attempt on His life (v. 28-29). Why? What happened?

Quite simply, their Jews-only or Nazareth-primarily claim to Jesus was refused by Him (v. 25-27), resulting in a Messiah who was different from the one they wanted. He wouldn't be limited to a first-century synagogue crowd, a twenty-first-century church crowd, or any other preferential circle that thinks itself uniquely entitled to Him. He was not only sent to their poor, their prisoners, their blind, and their oppressed (v. 18) but also to all others—to everyone who recognizes themselves to be afflicted by sin and its consequences. This means Jesus' ministry extends to some very messed-up lives and undesirable people groups.

Jesus likened His reign as Messiah to Israel's Year of Jubilee and called it the year or season "of the Lord's favor" (v. 19). According to the Old Testament (Leviticus 25:8-55), every fiftieth year was to signal God's rightful Lordship over everything and everyone, including the results of people's mistakes. Debts were to be canceled, property was to be returned, slaves were to be freed, and everyone was to enjoy miraculous blessings.

Jesus came to do all these things for us, but He also came to do the same things for others, including those who live very different lives from ours. Receiving His much-needed ministry ourselves requires embracing the other souls He came to rescue, heal, and restore. If we reject the reach of His ministry, then we reject Him (v. 24) because His vast reach is why He came.

Prayer: I celebrate the coming of the One who wishes to reach even the neediest of the needy. May I recognize any way in which I'm exclusive rather than inclusive in my view of others. May I have the insight to identify the imprisoned, the blind, and the oppressed—whether they live nearby or at great distances from me.

Notes:

___

___

___

___

___

___

___

___

___

___

Personal Prayer:

___

___

___

___

___

___

___

___

___

___

___

___

December 3

Let us go somewhere else—to the nearby villages—so I can preach there also. That is why I have come.

Mark 1:38 (from Mark 1:21-39)

(See also Luke 4:43 from Luke 4:31-44)

Let's Get a Couple Things Straight

It's difficult to envision a time and place with virtually no effective medical treatment. In such a setting, conditions that are minor to us would be major, even life-threatening. A cut, a broken bone, an infection could result in someone's death.

Across most of human history (and for scores of people still today), such perils were the reality of daily life. This was the case for everyone in first-century Palestine. Because people loved each other every bit as much as we love each other, the illnesses of friends and family members wrenched their hearts with utter despair.

Think about the impact of a miracle worker traveling the countryside—a healer of every medical ailment, a deliverer from every inexplicable demon. This is how Jesus came on the scene during His earthly ministry. A modern-day comparison might be to picture Him walking the halls of cancer treatment centers and children's hospitals, curing every patient. What a groundswell of euphoria and expectation would erupt as news of His abilities spread.

It was in the midst of such a surge of miracles that Jesus prioritized His reason for coming. One weekend, in the seaside community of Capernaum, after He delivered a disruptive demoniac (v. 21-28) and lifted a disciple's in-law from her sickbed (v. 29-31), the entire community brought their desperate ones to the miracle worker for Him to perform His miracles, which He did (v. 32-34).

The next morning, before daylight, Jesus found a solitary place outdoors to pray (v. 35). Being fully human, perhaps He needed to replenish His physical or emotional strength. Maybe He found the muzzling of demoniacs who boasted about knowing Him (v. 23-24, 34) or the people's crazed chasing after His powers distracting.

Whatever the focus of Jesus' prayers, when His disciples (and the crowd, according to Luke's account) located Him, their desire was for Him to return to what He'd been doing—performing miracles for the community (v. 36-37). Jesus' response signaled at least two priorities embedded in His reason for coming.

First, His gaze was upon additional locations (v. 38). Whereas our focus often remains on our own setting, Jesus came to reach the entire world and those far outside our realm of personal interest. Various high-visibility platforms could have provided Him with heights of fame, but He wished to travel to obscure places and reach tucked-away individuals. In addition to this, He repeatedly walked away from the already-reached to seek out the not-yet-reached.

Second, Jesus wanted to preach (v. 38). As urgent as we view our physical needs to be, He views our spiritual needs as far more serious. According to Luke's account, it was the "good news of the kingdom of God" that He wanted to preach (Luke 4:43), the same "good news of great joy that will be for all the people" that was heralded at His birth—the news that a Savior has arrived (Luke 2:10-11).

Yes, Jesus would continue to heal and perform other miracles. His ability to do so is part of the good news, but His spiritual ministry matters far more than His physical ministry because His spiritual ministry changes hearts and ushers people into eternity. Becoming the Savior is what Jesus wants to accomplish—both in our lives and in far-flung, tucked-away places. It's the reason He came.

Prayer: I celebrate the coming of the One who not only wishes to meet my needs but also the needs of others and who primarily wishes to meet spiritual needs. I ask for an increased awareness of the needs awaiting Jesus' ministry in the not-yet-reached lives of this world.

Notes:

___

___

___

___

___

___

___

___

___

Personal Prayer:

___

___

___

___

___

___

___

___

___

___

December 4

Do not think that I have come to abolish the Law or the Prophets; I have not come to abolish them but to fulfill them.

Matthew 5:17

We Have History Together

In a culture that thrives on change and newness, many things are short-lived rather than long-lasting. Too often disposability replaces durability. Consequently, very little is anchored securely enough in our past or our present to give us any assurance of it remaining in our future. How keenly we feel the absence of guaranteed continuity, whether it be in our relationships or other areas of our lives.

Not so with God. He is unchangeable across time and eternity. He says of His own character, "I the LORD do not change" (Malachi 3:6). He says of His love, "I have loved you with an everlasting love" (Jeremiah 31:3).

The moment sin entered the world through Adam and Eve, God's love announced His provision to rescue us from it (Genesis 3:15). Indeed, His gift of Jesus was fully in place, ready for Adam and Eve and ready for us, "from the creation of the world" (Revelation 13:8), which means before anyone lived or sinned.

Though God knew every awful detail of the sins we would commit (oh, think of it), a kingdom has been prepared for us "since the creation of the world" (Matthew 25:34). There are many ways that Jesus brings change and newness, but there are other ways in which everything about Him has been established since "before the world began" (John 17:5).

The Old Testament, known to the Jews as "the Law and the Prophets," recounts century after century, millennium after millennium of God preparing a people through whom Jesus was to be given to the world. It's not surprising, then, that He didn't come to make the Old Testament disposable but to step fully and perfectly into everything it teaches and promises about Him.

Some Old Testament decrees are ceremonial in nature, using symbolism and object lessons to teach truth to a people surrounded by error. For example, sacrifices for sin required unblemished animals and exacting procedures to convey the gravity of sin and the high cost of removing it. However, no amount of animals equals the value of even one human soul, so animal sacrifices didn't remove people's sins (Hebrews 10:1-14). What they did was serve as place markers until God's perfect, priceless sacrifice was offered for the whole world. Christians no longer practice the ceremonial aspects of the Old Testament, not because Jesus abolished them but because He thoroughly fulfilled them.

Other Old Testament decrees are moral in nature, such as are found in the Ten Commandments. Just as Jesus fulfilled all the ceremonial demands of the Old Testament by surpassing them, He did the same with its moral codes. In addition to living the only sinless life ever lived, He embodied such a thorough righteousness as to push beyond all external rules and fulfill God's loftiest desires. We practice the moral aspects of the Old Testament by inviting Jesus into our hearts to live in us and through us, fleshing out His righteousness with our every act of obedience to His prompting (2 Corinthians 5:21).

For thousands of years, the Old Testament prepared for and pointed toward the coming of the One who has loved us since before creation. If something or someone in our lives is uncertain or untrustworthy, Jesus isn't. He has a history with us that predates time itself; and He wants to have a future with us, a future that will last for all of eternity. It's why He came.

Prayer: I celebrate the coming of the One whose faithful involvement in my life has been orchestrated since before time began. Every day but especially when the people and possessions of my life seem less than stable and less than reliable, may I increasingly lean upon God's unchangeable love.

Notes:

Personal Prayer:

December 5

It is not the healthy who need a doctor, but the sick. I have not come to call the righteous, but sinners to repentance.

Luke 5:31-32 (from Luke 5:27-32)

(See also Matthew 9:12-13 from Matthew 9:9-13 and Mark 2:17 from Mark 2:13-17)

Bad Beginnings but Good Endings

The man who wrote one of the four Gospels, including the account of Gabriel visiting Joseph and the account of the Magi visiting Jesus, didn't have an impressive start. As a Jew, he should have been righteous, but he wasn't. A devout Jew wouldn't have worked for the Roman army collecting burdensome taxes from downtrodden countrymen, probably inflating the charges for his own selfish gain. Such behavior was so despised by other Jews that it was lumped together with that of robbers, prostitutes, pagans, and other extreme wrongdoers. This was Levi's beginning.

While Levi (also called Matthew) was in the very midst of his sinfulness, Jesus approached him and invited him to join God's kingdom (v. 27). His response was immediate and all-out (v. 28). He hosted a great banquet at his home in honor of Jesus (v. 29). It's predictable who attended—people just like him, namely, other tax collectors and "sinners." Indeed, they attended in large number (v. 29). This resulted in criticism from various religious officials (v. 30), which, in turn, led to Jesus' announcement about whom He was and wasn't calling into His kingdom (v. 31-32).

In order to sense the full impact of this occasion, it would help to project its details ahead 2,000 years and liken the banquet crowd to the most despised sinners of our day—people who have undesirable traits and messy lives, people whose sins seem particularly inexcusable as was the case for Levi and his guests. By eating with these people, Jesus embraced them so unreservedly that the religious establishment was sure He was wrong. After all, they weren't guilty of any of the things these people had done.

What a shock it must have been to hear Jesus say He came for such sinners as Levi and his friends rather than for the religious people who distanced themselves from these sinners. The reason is straightforward enough: just as a sick person acknowledges his need for a doctor, an admitted sinner acknowledges his need for a Savior. Even though all of us are sinners, if we think we're "good enough" because we behave better than someone else, then we deafen our hearts to Jesus' call. He calls sinners. We have to know that's who we are, or we fail to hear Him.

One of the best indicators of how we view ourselves is found in how we view others. A self-righteous person focuses upon all he or she does to lay claim to being righteous. By comparison, others seem more sinful, and this results in stepping back from them because of their sinfulness. In contrast, self-admitted sinners view others as fellow sinners with lives that are as needy as their own, and this results in stepping toward them with the embrace of Jesus who calls all sinners to repentance (v. 32).

The truth is, only Jesus is righteous enough to step back from sinners; yet He takes the biggest and most merciful steps toward them, even the worst of them. The truth is, He can save a sinner so completely as to use that person to write the lead book of the New Testament. And, the truth is, this is why He came—to turn bad beginnings into good endings for each of us.

Prayer: I celebrate the coming of the One who turns bad beginnings into good endings. Regardless of someone's sins, I want to fully believe in Jesus' embrace—enough to experience it myself and enough to extend it to others. I want to remain mindful enough of my own sinfulness to never step back from someone else's sinfulness.

Notes:

Personal Prayer:

December 6

Do not suppose that I have come to bring peace to the earth. I did not come to bring peace, but a sword.

Matthew 10:34 (from Matthew 10:34-39)

I have come to bring fire on the earth ... Do you think I came to bring peace on earth? No, I tell you, but division.

Luke 12:49,51 (from Luke 12:49-53)

A Line Across Christmas

These verses don't sound like the serene nativity scene that we envision nestled inside a Bethlehem stable. They don't sound like the angel's announcement of "good tidings of great joy" or the words from our favorite Christmas carol. A sword, fire, and division aren't inviting in the least. There's already enough turmoil in the world and in our own lives. These verses don't sound like anything that anyone wants from Jesus!

What they do sound like, however, is an accurate description of Jesus' earthly ministry. His teachings and miracles repeatedly produced division because some people followed Him while others rejected Him, preferring to remain in their sins. It wasn't the early believers who generated animosity toward unbelievers. On the rare occasions when this occurred, the believers were sternly rebuked by Jesus Himself (Luke 9:51-56; 22:47-51). Instead, it was unbelievers who resented the clear lines Jesus drew. They pulled back from Him, even lashing out at Him, and He warned His followers to expect similar treatment (John 15:18-21).

Jesus' ministry during the first century, across church history, and still today inevitably draws dividing lines—between those who receive Him and those who reject Him. He doesn't soften His message to ease this line. He boldly says of Himself: "I am the way and the truth and the life. No one comes to the Father except through me" (John 14:6). These are extremely offensive words to those who prefer a different message.

When the line that Jesus draws between belief and unbelief cuts through a family, then the slice of His sword and the flame of His fire are keenly felt. The division can fall between father and son or mother and daughter, as well as between other members of one's household. It's not that we as believers want or cause the division; Jesus would rebuke us if we did, just as He rebuked earlier disciples who were wrongfully critical or combative toward nonbelievers. But we must be willing to experience the division because it's His truth causing it. This is the "hating" (putting in second place) of others that He asks of us (Luke 14:25-33; Matthew 10:37).

Jesus Himself experienced division within His own earthly family. Early in His ministry, they viewed Him as crazy (Mark 3:21). On at least one occasion His brothers taunted Him with what seems like a willingness to endanger His life (John 7:1-5). It wasn't until after Jesus' death, resurrection, and ascension that His brothers were counted among the believers (Acts 1:14). During most of His earthly life, the very dividing line that Jesus drew cut deeply through His own family.

Why did Jesus come to bring division, to draw such a severe and potentially painful line across our world? Actually, it was already drawn, with sinful humanity on one side and God on the other side. Each of us drew this line of separation with our sins and destined ourselves to an eternity on the wrong side of the line separated from God.

This line, which Jesus came to affirm, He also came to bridge for everyone who accepts Him. When we accept Him, the line becomes a mark of where we were before Jesus. It reminds us that we've been separated from a life of sin and separated unto a life in fellowship with God. If we haven't yet experienced the drawing of this line, may it be drawn across our lives this Christmas season. It's the reason Jesus came.

> Prayer: I celebrate the coming of the One who bridges the line drawn between me and God. When Jesus' teaching results in a line between those who accept Him and those who reject Him, painful as such lines are, I rejoice in the reminder that He's the One who bridges the lines that our sins draw.

Notes:

Personal Prayer:

December 7

For I have come down from heaven not to do my will but to do the will of him who sent me. And this is the will of him who sent me, that I shall lose none of all that he has given me, but raise them up at the last day.

John 6:38

Mission Possible

If anyone ever deserved to exercise personal will, it was Jesus. In addition to being fully God, He was sinless and perfect in every aspect of His humanity. Surely these qualifications would have generated inclinations that were acceptable to pursue.

Yet, Jesus didn't follow His own will, not ever. The all-knowing One didn't self-produce His words; instead, He received them from God the Father (John 12:49). The all-powerful One didn't self-produce His deeds; instead, He committed Himself to receiving them from the Father (John 5:19). Even when the wrongs of others threatened to harm Him, He placed His Father's will above His own desires (Luke 22:42).

With far less to endorse our own personal preferences, we're prone to choose our will over God's will repeatedly. We opt for choices that seem attractive and beneficial, but in reality, we're being deceived (Genesis 3:6). When situations are perplexing or difficult, we rely on our best guesses even though our wisdom is faulty (Proverbs 26:12). We fear that following God's will might make us look foolish, even though His understanding far exceeds ours and is without limits (Psalm 147:5).

What was so compelling about the will of God the Father as to capture Jesus' every interest and intention? A mission—one that gave Him such joy as to cause everything else to matter less (Hebrews 12:2). Jesus' life was all about accomplishing this mission, the most God-ordained mission that has ever existed.

Jesus' mission involved a sending by God the Father, a coming by God the Son, and an anointing by God the Spirit. In other words, what the Father initiated, the Son was willing to accomplish, and the Spirit made possible. Only as the desires and workings of the entire Godhead functioned in perfect harmony was this monumental undertaking brought to completion.

A similar display of divine collaboration was present in creation. Father, Son, and Spirit are credited by Scripture for the events of Genesis 1 and 2 (1 Corinthians 8:6; Colossians 1:15-16; Genesis 1:2). Then, as soon as Genesis 3, when sin spoiled all of it, the Godhead united in the sending, coming, and anointing of the One who would re-create everything.

Accomplishing the mission of delivering us from earth to heaven is why Jesus came. His readiness to sacrifice His will for the will of the One who sent Him invites us to do the same (John 13:15). This isn't an invitation to a life of deprivation or drudgery but a life of such love and joy as to be comparable to the love and joy Jesus Himself experiences in relationship with His Father (John 15:9-11).

Amazing as it is, we matter enough to God for all of the Godhead to join in our spiritual rescue from sin. We matter enough for the Son of God to sacrifice His everything for us. There's no greater assurance that a mission will be accomplished than for "all of God" to be committed to its accomplishment. Those who fully believe in the One who was sent (John 6:29) will be delivered for all of eternity to the One who sent Him (John 6:38). Jesus came to accomplish this, and He will accomplish it—not just for others but for us too.

> Prayer: I celebrate the coming of the One who will accomplish the mission He was sent to accomplish, not only in others' lives but also in my life. At times when I question my spiritual destiny, I will rely upon Jesus delivering me from earth to heaven for all of eternity.

Notes:

Personal Prayer:

December 8

For the Son of Man came to seek and to save what was lost.

Luke 19:10 (from Luke 19:1-10)

(Also said in Matthew 18:11 and Luke 9:56)

Someone Is After Us

Perhaps the only way a person could have been viewed as more sinful and despised than Levi (see December 5) would be if he were a "chief" tax collector like Zacchaeus (v. 2). As the supervisor of an entire district of tax collectors, Zacchaeus would have been seasoned and skillful in his awful activities. This is evidenced by the extent of his ill-gotten gain (v. 2). And, like Levi, being a Jew made Zacchaeus' wrongs seem all the more inexcusable.

How interesting that Jesus approached such a "super-sinner" as Levi at the beginning of His earthly ministry and Zacchaeus, similar but even worse, toward the end of His earthly ministry. These two strategically placed encounters make a clear statement about Jesus' mission. On both occasions, He chose to engage in the familiarity of dining at the sinner's home, making His embrace of the outcast even more pronounced. And, on both occasions, this was met with immediate criticism (v. 7) from those who viewed themselves as better and more deserving than such blatant wrongdoers.

Not only were Jesus' actions clear; His words were equally clear: He came to seek and to save lost people. That's who Zacchaeus was—a lost person. Perhaps he thought of himself as anything but lost since his chosen path had led to considerable success by worldly standards. Spiritually, however, he was lost. Jesus knew this and cared enough to do something about it.

It might seem sufficient that Jesus was only weeks away from dying for Zacchaeus, paying the ultimate price of His own life so that He could save Zacchaeus from the consequences his sins deserved. But Jesus is not only the One who saves us; He's also the One who seeks us. He came to do both. He did both for Zacchaeus, and He does both for us.

Zacchaeus was curious about who or what had caused the crowd (v. 3-4). That's all, just curious about the commotion. Jesus was the seeker, not Zacchaeus. In one of the largest, most bustling cities of first-century Palestine and in the midst of a crowd whose size and intensity must have been considerable, Jesus called Zacchaeus out by name and asked to enter his world (v. 5). He's done the very same for each of us. We've heard His voice in our hearts, and we've felt His request to enter our lives. Rightly so, since He came to seek and save lost people, and that's who we are.

Jesus referred to Himself as the Son of Man in this statement, a verse that many scholars mark as the theme verse of Luke. Of course, the Christmas miracle is that He's both the Son of God and the Son of Man, fully God and fully man. But Jesus' favorite name for Himself was Son of Man. He called Himself this far more than any other title. He preferred to emphasize His humanity because He came to be one of us—to walk among us, to experience what we experience, to feel what we feel. That's who seeks us out, One who truly understands (Hebrews 4:15).

In response to this amazing Jesus, Zacchaeus went from curiosity and hospitality to genuine repentance and zealous commitment. For his type of wrongdoing, the Old Testament required a 120% correction (Leviticus 6:1-5). Instead, Zacchaeus offered 400% to everyone he had ever wronged, plus half of everything he had for the poor (v. 8). This drastic change in character shows that his Seeker became his Savior, making the outcast Jew a true Jew (v. 9). The Old Testament required one other thing—a sacrifice on the altar (Leviticus 6:6-7). In just a few weeks Jesus would lay down His life to be that sacrifice, for Zacchaeus and for us. He seeks us in our sins to save us from our sins. This is why He came.

Prayer: I celebrate the coming of the One who not only came to save sinners but also came to seek them out, including the worst ones. That's who I am, a sinner who needs Jesus' seeking and saving. I respond to Him with genuine repentance for my sins and zealous commitment to His Lordship.

Notes:

Personal Prayer:

December 9

For judgment I have come into this world, so that the blind will see and those who see will become blind.

John 9:39 (from John 9:1-41)

Can You See Him Now?

Of all Jesus' recorded miracles, the most frequently performed was the healing of blind eyes—probably because physical blindness serves as an analogy for spiritual blindness. All sinners walk in the spiritual blindness that's caused by sin. Old Testament prophets announced repeatedly that the Messiah would heal blindness and restore sight, referring primarily to people's spiritual vision. The light of the world would come to end its darkness.

To emphasize Jesus' ability to heal spiritual blindness, He healed physical blindness over and over again. The lengthiest and most intriguing account is found in John 9. A person couldn't be any blinder than if they were born that way (v. 1) and couldn't be any more affected by blindness than to be reduced to begging (v. 8). This worst-case scenario was used to showcase God's ability to work wonders in someone's life (v. 3). The parallel truth is that He's equally capable of working spiritual wonders, even for the most extreme, debased sinner.

How Jesus healed this man is meaningful. The One who formed the first eyes from the "dust of the ground" (Genesis 2:7) reached into that same dust to restore eyesight (v. 6-7). Clearly, He who first made us is fully capable of remaking us, even if our need is the worst imaginable. Jesus' absolute authority as Creator was further proclaimed by how intentionally and frequently

He healed people on the Sabbath, including this man. Only the One who rested from the work of creation on the seventh day (Genesis 2:1-3) had the right to reveal Himself by works of re-creation on the same day (v. 14).

The skepticism surrounding the miracle reveals a stubborn refusal to see Jesus for who He really is. The religious leaders, who should have had good spiritual eyesight, preferred to remain blind rather than see Jesus as God. Back and forth the arguments went until the man and his miracle were barred from their midst (v. 34). Left without the leadership of those who should have led him the right way, Jesus went after the man to add spiritual sight to his physical sight (v. 35).

On other occasions, Jesus seemed to say the opposite of what He said on this occasion regarding being our judge (v. 39). He said He wasn't sent and didn't come to judge or condemn the world but to save the world (John 3:17; 12:47). This is true, proven by the experience of all of us who deserve judgment for sin but instead receive forgiveness and salvation. Today is the "day" or season of opportunity for salvation (2 Corinthians 6:2), not only for the blind man but for us too. This season was ushered in by Jesus' coming. It's on the "last day" that He will conduct judgment (John 12:48), a role assigned to Him by the Father (John 5:22; Acts 10:42).

However, if we prefer our sinful darkness to Jesus' light and thereby reject God's provision of salvation, as did this man's interrogators, then our future judgment is already decided and it's decided by us (John 3:18). This is the judgment that accompanied Jesus' coming. Revealing who He is draws a distinction between those who presume to see but are actually blind versus those who acknowledge their blindness and want Jesus to restore their sight.

If we deny our spiritual blindness, claiming we see well enough to guide our own life, we're left in our blindness. But, if we acknowledge our need for Jesus to remake how we see everything, including how we see our sin and His salvation, then He restores our spiritual sight. To accomplish this is why He came.

Prayer: I celebrate the coming of the One who is able to heal spiritual blindness. Only my Creator is capable of re-creating me after sin distorts my vision and darkens my path. During this season of salvation, I invite Him on a daily basis to remake how I see everything.

Notes:

Personal Prayer:

December 10

I have come that they may have life, and have it to the full.

John 10:10 (from John 10:1-16)

Neither Half Empty Nor Half Full

In direct response to someone who was treated wrongly by those claiming to be religious (John 9), Jesus announced something noteworthy: He's not like bogus shepherds who harm their flock by putting personal interests above the sheep's needs. Instead, He's "the good shepherd" (v. 11,14). In first-century Palestine, this title was packed with meaning, both culturally and spiritually. It reached back to the description of God penned by Israel's shepherd-king David: "The LORD is my shepherd" (Psalm 23:1).

That's who Jesus was claiming to be, the One David trusted and worshiped. Unlike illegitimate caretakers who use questionable approaches to access the sheep, Jesus enters rightfully through the sheepfold's gate because He's the real shepherd (v. 1-2). Ownership of His sheep is further evidenced by His naming each of them and by their recognizing His voice and following His lead (v. 3-4).

When Jesus' audience didn't fully comprehend His analogy (v. 6), His clarification intensified His claims. As the good shepherd, He also serves as the sheepfold's gate (v. 7). It was customary for a shepherd to position himself at the pen's opening when he led the flock back from a day of grazing. He did this to make sure all the sheep returned to the fold's safety, to inspect them for injuries, and to treat their wounds. Then, for the flock's protection, he placed his body across the gate during the night, until he called each one out by name the next day.

In sharp contrast to someone whose desires are self-serving and whose intentions result in our destruction, Jesus offers us, His sheep, absolute and eternal safety (v. 9). Indeed, as our shepherd, He would lay down His life to make possible our spiritual wellbeing (v. 11). He offers this relationship of protection and intimacy not only to Israel but also to the entire world (v. 14-16). Day after day, He leads His sheep in and out of the fold to enjoy nourishing pasture (v. 9).

The best description that Shepherd Jesus could give for what He provides is to say He gives us life—specifically, the fullest, most abundant and vibrant version of life (v. 10). He's not just referring to eternity; He's also describing His provision for our earthly lives. The One who will be our life-giving shepherd in heaven (Revelation 7:17) is already our life-giving shepherd. Who better to offer life at such an ultimate level than the One who created and sustains all life (Colossians 1:16-17)?

The question is, do we really view our relationship with Jesus in this way? Satan suggests that God withholds good things from us, things that would make our lives better if we but reach for them (Genesis 3:1-6). Consequently, all too often, Christianity is defined as an exercise in denying oneself all the zesty aspects of life, when nothing could be further from the truth.

Could it be that the world has an anemic view of Christianity because so many of us live an anemic version of it? How tragic, both for us and for others! The new life that Jesus came to make available begins the moment someone is born again, and it's a life of intimacy (v. 14-15) as well as a life "to the full" (v. 10). He came to make sure it's ours to enjoy.

Prayer: I celebrate the coming of the One who wants to shepherd me into the fullest life possible. I need Him to treat my wounds and provide my protection. I want to listen for His voice directing me into the pasture He identifies as rich and nourishing. I want Him with me day and night.

Notes:

_____

_____

_____

_____

_____

_____

_____

_____

_____

_____

Personal Prayer:

_____

_____

_____

_____

_____

_____

_____

_____

_____

_____

_____

_____

December 11

[The] Son of Man did not come to be served, but to serve, and to give his life as a ransom for many.

Matthew 20:28 (from Matthew 20:17-28)

(See also Mark 10:45 from Mark 10:35-45)

Climbing the Ladder Downward

Jesus had just explained in graphic terms the suffering He was about to endure (v. 17-19); but the thoughts of at least two disciples were still on His earlier mention of thrones, glory, and blessings (Matthew 19:28-30). Not only were those words more attractive, but they aligned better with everything taught by first-century Jewish leaders about the coming Messiah. They said He would overthrow the occupying Roman government and reestablish Israel's supremacy as an independent nation.

The sons of Zebedee, James and John, didn't want to miss their rightful role in such a kingdom, nor did their mother want them to miss out (v. 20). A combining of Matthew's and Mark's accounts indicates that the three of them petitioned Jesus together. They requested the positions of highest power, prominence, and prestige for these two fishermen turned followers (v. 21).

Luke adds that none of the disciples understood what Jesus had just said about His impending arrest and death, that "they did not know what he was talking about" (Luke 18:34). Thinking only in terms of an earthly kingdom and being slow to comprehend a spiritual kingdom, however, doesn't excuse self-centered, self-seeking aspirations. After following Jesus for approximately three years and witnessing His amazing abilities, James and John wanted to be sure they received sufficient advancement from Him.

This isn't so different from the crowds who chased Jesus for bread (John 6:26) or similar blessing seekers today. Also, it's much like modern ministers who bask in the attention and acclaim afforded by a platform. James and John, along with Peter, were already privileged to comprise Jesus' inner circle of friends (Matthew 26:37; Mark 5:37; Luke 8:51). Sadly, though, it wasn't increased intimacy that His disciples requested.

How mistaken these two brothers were about their own merits. They assured Jesus that they could qualify regardless of the criteria (v. 22). But, both of them, far from being ready to suffer, would run when their Master was arrested (Matthew 26:56) and hide when He was crucified (John 20:19).

Despite these early deficiencies, Jesus prophesied that James and John would indeed suffer for Him in the future (v. 23). James would be the first of the twelve to be martyred for his faith, bludgeoned to death by a sword (Acts 12:2). John, perhaps as old as 90, would be banished to an island of rock sixty miles offshore to labor in prison quarries (Revelation 1:9). What changed them and qualified them? Among other things, perhaps it was Jesus' instruction on this very occasion.

With the other ten disciples indignant (v. 24), probably jealous because two of them requested what all of them wanted, Jesus explained genuine greatness. Like us, the disciples were surrounded by wrong examples (v. 25), so He offered His own example: the path to spiritual greatness is servanthood (v. 26). Only by walking lowly levels do we ever walk lofty levels (v. 27). Then and only then does the One in charge of promotion decide placement (v. 23).

Jesus expects His right example to outweigh a world of wrong examples because only His example sacrificed everything, His very life, to buy us back from living in wrong ways (v. 28). He came to be the ultimate example of servanthood so that we, too, can become servants, climbing downward rather than upward.

Prayer: I celebrate the coming of the One who set the example for how we are to live by how He lived. Rather than seeking the accolades of earthly kingdoms, I choose to live according to His kingdom. Rather than seeking the world's version of greatness, I choose the genuine greatness that's marked by serving others.

Notes:

Personal Prayer:

December 12

Now my heart is troubled, and what shall I say? "Father, save me from this hour"? No, it was for this very reason I came to this hour. Father, glorify your name!

John 12:27-28 (from John 12:20-28)

What Time Is It?

The Gospel of John records Jesus' earthly ministry along a plot line of references to "the hour" and "the time." It starts as early as Jesus' unusual response to His mother in connection with His first miracle: "My time has not yet come" (John 2:4). It continues throughout the book, almost as if a cosmic clock can be heard ticking.

Repeatedly, Jesus (or John) indicates that His hour/time is yet ahead or is still coming (John 2:4; 4:21; 5:28-29; 7:6; 7:8; 7:30; 8:20). Sometimes there are references to the hour/time having partially arrived but being in the future in its fullest form (John 4:23; 5:25).

All of this changes, however, at a pivotal point in John 12 when we suddenly read, "The hour has come" (v. 23). What hour? Toward what precise point in human history was a divine clock moving? Jesus provides the answer: "The hour has come for the Son of Man to be glorified" (v. 23).

But hadn't Jesus' glory been visible before this moment? With His first miracle, we read, "He thus revealed his glory" (John 2:11), even though it wasn't time for a full revelation (John 2:4). As His miracles continued, it's safe to assume His glory continued to be revealed, at least partially. Then, in a most climatic miracle, His friend Lazarus was allowed to die so that, by calling him forth from the tomb, God's glory would be exceedingly evident, thereby, glorifying Jesus (John 11:4).

These glimpses of glory might strike us as plenty impressive, but a clock was advancing toward a revelation of much greater glory. It wouldn't be displayed by turning water into wine or by calling a man back from death. Jesus' words in John 12 make it clear: ultimate glory would be displayed by His suffering on the cross for our sins. After all, what's more glorious than a God who would give His life to eliminate our death?

Jesus would become a kernel of wheat falling to the ground and dying to produce many seeds (v. 24). He would be the one to "hate" His life (love it less) in order to pave the path to eternity (v. 25). He would serve us so that He could invite us to serve Him (v. 26).

No one realized it at the time, but this is the glory the angels announced to the shepherds—that Jesus was born for us in order to die for us, thus, showing God at His greatest (Luke 2:14). Supreme glory wouldn't be displayed by God's power or authority. It would be displayed by the servanthood and suffering of His love.

Immediately upon Judas leaving to betray Jesus to His enemies, Jesus said, "Now is the Son of Man glorified and God is glorified in Him" (John 13:31). With His arrest imminent, He prayed, "Father, the time has come. Glorify your son, that your Son may glorify you" (John 17:1). As amazing as the resurrection and ascension would be, the crucifixion showcased God's ultimate glory because it showcased His love.

What triggered the arrival of the hour in John 12? It seems like an insignificant detail that's easily overlooked, but what had just happened was the arrival of Gentiles seeking Jesus (v. 20-22). That's when He said, "The hour has come" (v. 23) because the Father's love had sent Him not only for Israel but for the whole world (John 3:16).

Was it tempting for Jesus to resist servanthood and suffering? Indeed it was (v. 27), as it is for any of us. However, the baby was placed in Bethlehem for a reason: to display God's glorious love to the world. That's why Jesus came.

Prayer: I celebrate the coming of the One who provided the ultimate display of God's glory not with power or authority but with self-sacrifice for me. When I wonder if God is great enough for something or loving enough for someone, I'll listen for the cosmic clock ticking away toward His clearest showing of who He is.

Notes:

Personal Prayer:

December 13

I have come into the world as a light, so that no one who believes in me should stay in darkness.

John 12:46 (from John 12:37-46)

Plug in the Lights

Few things are as closely associated with the celebration of Christmas as light. From the soft glow of candles to the twinkling strands on trees, to decorate for Christmas almost always includes displays of light. Perhaps this is because the Bible associates Jesus' coming with light. Perhaps, as well, it's an acknowledgment of how dark our lives would be without the light that He brought.

Light is so characteristic of God, so essential to His "God-ness" that He's said to be light (1 John 1:5), just as He's said to be spirit (John 4:24) and to be love (1 John 4:8,16). Indeed, His first creative act was to issue forth light (Genesis 1:3), almost as if this expression of Himself had to be first. Only as His light shines forth, can His splendor and purposes be seen.

Repeatedly, however, the Bible refers to the darkening effects of sin, both upon an individual and upon the entire world. The more we sin, the further we walk away from God, our only source of light, consequently, the more darkness we enter. We may claim our self-chosen path is clever and right, but all the while we're stumbling blindly (Proverbs 4:19) toward an eternity of darkness (Matthew 8:12).

Jesus began His earthly ministry by stepping into a 700-year-old prophecy from Isaiah: "the people living in darkness have seen a great light; on those living in the land of the shadow of death a light has dawned" (Isaiah 9:2 as quoted in Matthew 4:16). For everyone who walks in the darkness produced by personal sin, for everyone who walks in the ever-encroaching shadow of eternal death, a light has dawned, a great light—Jesus.

Jesus said of Himself: "I am the light of the world. Whoever follows me will never walk in darkness, but will have the light of life" (John 8:12). Just as darkness and death are closely associated, so are light and life. The source and giver of life, Jesus, "became flesh and made his dwelling among us" (John 1:14), shining His light on the darkness of our sinfulness so that we could step out of it into His light and life.

Surely everyone would heartily welcome this opportunity, wouldn't they? After all, we enjoy all the festive Christmas lights that celebrate Jesus' coming. However, Jesus' light exposes sin, and, because of this, many people prefer to remain in their darkness (John 3:19-20). They don't want to be confronted or corrected or changed. They mistakenly think sin provides wonderful, worthwhile living while their Creator withholds it from them. They don't trust Jesus enough to exchange their darkness for His light.

Once we enter Jesus' light and life, we leave behind us the darkness and death of our sinful lives. This doesn't mean we become perfect. What it does mean is that we've been made "a new creation" (2 Corinthians 5:17) and we're walking in a new direction on a path of light that keeps getting brighter and brighter (Proverbs 4:18).

If we're tempted to allow room for certain sins in our lives, we must not do so. Jesus' presence is to shine in our hearts (2 Corinthians 4:6), His Word is to illuminate our steps (Psalm 119:105), and our lives are to give light to others in a darkened world (Matthew 5:14-16). This is why Jesus came—so that we no one has to live in darkness. May every sparkle of a Christmas light remind us that He came to turn darkness into light.

Prayer: I celebrate the coming of the One who came to light up this dark world by lighting up individual dark lives. Every day, every moment, I invite the brilliance of Jesus' light to illuminate both my sins and my steps. May each twinkle of a Christmas light remind me that His light walks me into His life.

Notes:

Personal Prayer:

December 14

Jesus answered, "You are right in saying I am a king. In fact, for this reason I was born, and for this I came into the world, to testify to the truth."

John 18:37 (from John 18:28-19:1)

Some Things Aren't Up for Discussion or Negotiation

Peculiar as it might seem to read passages surrounding Jesus' death in a devotional about His birth, this devotional is about the entirety of His coming, which includes His birth, His death, and, most certainly, His true identity.

If Jesus were merely a man, then, outstanding as He may have been, we'd have every right to dismiss Him, in part or in whole. We could opt to let someone else direct our life. Or, we could opt to chart our own course. If He's simply one god among many gods or one of multiple paths to God, then, again, the choice is ours. We might argue that another god or another path suits us better.

However, if the One who stood before the Roman governor Pilate (v. 28-29) was really "Immanuel, which means 'God with us,'" as was announced to Joseph (Matthew 1:23), then He's not only a king but <u>the</u> King of all kings and <u>the</u> Lord of all lords (Revelation 17:14). He came to a nation (Luke 1:32-33) and to an entire world (John 1:10-11) that were already His rightful possession to rule.

So, Pilate had cause for concern, right? As did Herod years earlier at Jesus' birth? Both were regional rulers appointed with the primary responsibility of safeguarding the reign of Caesar over the Roman Empire in their assigned locations. Within their jurisdictions were the people of Israel who believed their Messiah would overthrow all outside powers and reestablish them as a great, independent nation.

Despite this popular expectation, Jesus explained that His throne didn't target Jerusalem or Rome or any other political capital of that day or our day. He told Pilot, "My kingdom is not of this world" (v. 36), because it's a spiritual kingdom established in human hearts. Jesus came to be the King of our lives. This throne, as well, is His rightful possession. It was invaded and captured by sin and its awful consequences. Jesus came to rescue us from enemy occupation and restore us to kingdom living and kingdom blessings.

There were other aspects of Jesus' kingship that were foreign to Pilate. Throughout history, kings have expected their subjects to serve them, even to die for them. But King Jesus served us and died for us. Never has there been nor will there be a king like this King. The greatest of heaven became the lowliest of earth, and He did it for us—because He loves us.

Jesus also told Pilate that He came to testify to truth, including the truth about His identity. To this, Pilate responded rather philosophically: "What is truth?" (v. 38) In other words, can truth really be known? Again, the assumption is that it's debatable or self-determined. If this is the case, then anything can be truth, anything Pilate wished or anything we wish. However, God's Word silences such notions. Jesus is identified as the One who "speaks the words of God" (John 3:31-34), which means He speaks ultimate, authoritative truth about us and Himself.

It's amazing that Jesus is described in Scripture as standing at the door of our hearts, knocking for entrance (Revelation 3:20). The King of the universe, the King of heaven, the King of eternity—awaiting an invitation into the kingdom of our individual lives. There's no better time than Christmas to let Him enter to rule with His love and truth because that's why He came.

Prayer: I celebrate the coming of the One who is the source of ultimate, authoritative truth as well as the rightful ruler over all thrones. Though He stands in a swirl of worldly opinions and debates about who He is, I want Him to rule every aspect of my life because I know who He is: God with us.

Notes:

Personal Prayer:

The Second Half—How Jesus Came

The Bible explains in the elegant language of the King James Version, "But when the fulness of time was come, God sent forth his Son" (Galatians 4:4). In other words, when the unfolding plan of God for the redemption of humanity converged at the perfect point in human history, the timing was exactly right for Jesus' arrival.

Of course, from a twenty-first-century perspective, much about the timing seems archaic and unfavorable. There was no media to announce the birth, no microphone to broadcast its significance, and no conveniences to make it comfortable. Yet, the Creator of an intricate and vast universe orchestrated every detail of Jesus' coming according to His wishes. With a divine hand upon the time and place and conditions, these aspects take on considerable meaning. It's as if "why" Jesus came was authenticated by "how" He came.

How Jesus came mattered to God. For this reason alone, how He came should matter to us as well. So, the second portion of this devotional invites the reader to spend the remainder of the Advent season pondering scene after scene of the biblical account of Jesus' arrival.

December 15

I will put enmity between you and the woman, and between your offspring and hers; he will crush your head, and you still strike his heel.

The Lord had said to Abram, "Leave your country, your people and your father's household and go to the land I will show you. I will make you into a great nation and I will bless you; I will make your name great and you will be a blessing ... and all peoples on earth will be blessed though you."

Then God said, "Yes, but your wife Sarah will bear you a son, and you will call him Isaac. I will establish my covenant with him as an everlasting covenant for his descendants after him."

All peoples on earth will be blessed through you and your offspring.

The scepter will not depart from Judah, nor the ruler's staff from between his feet, until he comes to whom it belongs and the obedience of the nation is his.

Genesis 3:15; 12:1-3; 17:19; 28:14; 49:10

Someone Keeps Promises

It's a humbling but comforting truth that nothing in our lives catches God by surprise, including our sins. Because He's eternally all-knowing, He knew about Adam and Eve's choice to sin before they were created, just as He knew about each of our sins before we were born. What a commitment of love God displays when He gives us life despite everything He knows we'll do with it.

Out of this amazing commitment, the provision of God's Son to purchase us back from our sinfulness was already in place before the first sin occurred (Revelation 13:8). Satan, who is not all-knowing, must have enjoyed his victory over Adam and Eve, convincing them to let sin enter the world. But, as soon as God approached them and provided a temporary remedy, He announced that a perfect, eternal provision was coming for their sins and ours.

He warned that human history would be plagued by hostility between Satan's offspring, probably referring to those who oppose God, and Eve's offspring, those who honor God (3:15). However, a singular offspring of Eve was promised. Satan would manage a heel-striking blow against Him, but He would render the final, fatal blow by crushing Satan's head (3:15). This becomes the first of many Old Testament prophecies of Jesus' coming.

In the unfolding of God's plan, He chose a couple, Abraham and Sarah, to give the miracle of a son, Isaac, in their old age. To Isaac and his wife, God gave two sons, Esau and Jacob. To Jacob, God gave twelve sons, who would become leaders of the tribes of Israel. At each juncture, God made a covenant—first to Abraham (12:1-3), later to Isaac (17:19), and later yet to Jacob (28:14). He promised to raise up a great nation through their lineage, a nation who would be His people in special ways; and He promised that this people would be used to bless the entire world.

With Jacob's twelve sons in place, one of them, Judah, was chosen by God to provide the lineage through whom a lasting reign would be placed over Israel (49:10). Hundreds of years later, Israel's King David, a descendant of Judah, began the dynasty. Later still, almost two thousand years after the promise to Judah, Jesus culminated the dynasty with His everlasting reign.

What started with the sin of two became the sin of all of us. What started with the promise to a couple became the promise to all of us. God has made provision through the gift of the Promised One to pay the full penalty for our sins and buy us back from spiritual death. No one's sins are too much—neither in amount nor severity. God made a promise in the opening chapters of Genesis to send a Savior and Lord, and He has kept that loving promise.

When Joseph and Mary traveled to Bethlehem to register as members of the "house and line of David" (Luke 2:4), a chord of faithfulness reached all the way back through time to God's promise about a scepter that wouldn't leave the tribe of Judah (49:10). The same chord of faithfulness reached back even further to promises made to Jacob, Isaac, and Abraham about their offspring blessing the whole world. And, it reached back further still to Adam and Eve who were promised an offspring who would be victor over sin.

How did Jesus come to earth? He came wrapped in the faithfulness of a God who loves us despite our sin and proves it by keeping His promises.

> Prayer: I celebrate the coming of the One who proves God loves us enough to keep His promises to us, despite our sinfulness. Even if I must wait days or decades for one of God's promises to be kept, I'll trust in His faithfulness because He's proven Himself across hundreds and thousands of years.

Notes:

Personal Prayer:

December 16

For unto us a child is born, to us a son is given, and the government will be on his shoulders. And he will be called Wonderful Counselor, Mighty God, Everlasting Father, Prince of Peace. Of the increase of his government and peace there will be no end. He will reign on David's throne and over his kingdom, establishing and upholding it with justice and righteousness from that time on and forever. The zeal of the LORD will accomplish this.

Isaiah 9:6-7

Check Out These Credentials

William Shakespeare is credited with penning a question: "What's in a name?" At least two thousand years before the playwright, Isaiah more than answered this inquiry with his prophecy about the coming Messiah.

God's plan debuts modestly enough with the birth of a child, the gift of a son (v. 6). Because He wouldn't be just any child or any son, the rest of the sentence is possible—the government would be on His shoulders (v.6). What government? The throne and kingdom of Israel's King David (v. 7), which was a dynasty God said would last forever (2 Samuel 7:16).

Of course, no one knew better than the prophet Isaiah that the nation of Israel had divided into two kingdoms. By Isaiah's day, the northern tribes were defeated and exiled, and the southern tribes would soon experience the same devastating fate for the same reason—the people's sinfulness. So, again, what government would rest on the Messiah's shoulders?

The answer is, the spiritual kingdom of God that David's reign symbolized. It would extend far beyond the borders of Palestine into human hearts around the world and across the centuries. The Coming One would reign on that throne, qualified not only by being David's rightful heir but also by holding additional credentials that Isaiah identified with five titles.

He would be "Wonderful" (v. 6). This isn't a descriptor of another title but is itself a title because it's a noun in the Hebrew text rather than an adjective. He would be a wonder. Indeed, He would be full of wonder. If this refers to His amazing power, then the next title of "Counselor" (v. 6) refers to His amazing knowledge and wisdom. Whereas earthly kings must surround themselves with counselors, this King would be the supreme Counselor.

The Apostle Paul combines these same two traits in describing Jesus as "the power of God and the wisdom of God (1 Corinthians 1:24). Not surprisingly, then, the third title affirms the deity of this all-powerful, all-knowing One—"Mighty God" (v. 6). And, underscoring the perfect unity of the Godhead, He is called "Everlasting Father" (v. 6), reminding us of Jesus' words: "I and the Father are one" (John 10:30).

If these titles are intended to build from one to the next, then the culminating one is striking: "Prince of Peace" (v. 6). Further, the increase of His peace would have no end (v. 7). Only this King could remove the cause of all turmoil and conflict—sin. By doing this, He would make peace possible, both among us and between each of us and God.

The gentle emphasis in the opening of this passage ought not to be overlooked. This gift of the five-titled Son is "unto us" (v. 6). He is for us, each of us, all of us. There's an additional truth embedded in the use of the present tense to refer to something that was seven hundred years away when Isaiah prophesied it: "a child is born … a son is given" (v. 6). Time doesn't define an eternal God. The gift has always been in place.

Upon taking His rightful throne over the kingdom of God, the Coming One would rule forever thereafter with justice and righteousness (v. 7). These two features are missing from so many earthly outcomes, but the zeal of the LORD Almighty ensures their accomplishment in the eternal kingdom and, until then, in the daily behavior of kingdom citizens.

How would the Coming One come? With a range and depth of kingly qualifications like no one else has ever had: Wonderful, Counselor, Mighty God, Everlasting Father, Prince of Peace.

Prayer: I celebrate the coming of the One whose credentials qualify Him to reign over the kingdom of my heart. I especially invite Him to exercise the rule of His peace, despite any turmoil that might loom and threaten me. With Jesus on the throne of my life, I'll extend justice and righteousness to others.

Notes:

Personal Prayer:

December 17

Who has believed our message and to whom has the arm of the LORD been revealed? He grew up before him like a tender shoot, and like a root out of dry ground. He had no beauty or majesty to attract us to him, nothing in his appearance that we should desire him. He was despised and rejected by men, a man of sorrows, and familiar with suffering. Like one from whom men hide their faces he was despised, and we esteemed him not. Surely he took up our infirmities and carried our sorrows, yet we considered him stricken by God, smitten by him and afflicted. But he was pierced for our transgressions, he was crushed for our iniquities; the punishment that brought us peace was upon him, and by his wounds we are healed. We all, like sheep, have gone astray, each of us has turned to his own way; and the LORD has laid on him the iniquity of us all. He was oppressed and afflicted, yet he did not open his mouth; he was led like a lamb to the slaughter, and as a sheep before her shearers is silent, so he did not open his mouth.

Isaiah 53:1-7 (from Isaiah 53:1-12)

Is It Really Him?

As un-Christmas-y as this passage sounds, perhaps no Old Testament prophecy about Jesus' coming is as extensive. The prophet Isaiah already had announced that a shoot would come forth from the stump of King David's father, Jesse (Isaiah 11:1). Here he clarifies that this tender growth would grow out of utter dryness (v. 2), in other words, from no expectation of fertility.

Though the Jews faithfully confessed their hope of a Messiah, it would have been hard to envision His coming. By the first century, it was more than five hundred years since the royal dynasty ceased its reign and the nation ceased its existence. The land and people of that bygone kingdom had become a weak, minuscule territory ruled by one of the greatest powers the world has ever known, the Roman Empire.

There would be additional "unlikely" aspects to King Jesus. In contrast to His ancestor, David, who was striking in appearance (1 Samuel 16:12,18), Isaiah foretold a King who would be the opposite: not handsome, not majestic, in no way attractive (v. 2). Rather than being welcomed and applauded, He would be despised and rejected, to the point of people turning their faces away from Him (v. 3).

A New Testament counterpart to this Old Testament prophecy is found in the opening words of the Gospel of John: "He came to that which was his own, but his own did not receive him" (John 1:11). It was His throne and

His kingdom. Indeed, the whole world is rightfully His by being its Creator, but it's left to human hearts to accept or reject Him.

Rather than exhibiting the splendor typically associated with royalty, King Jesus would be known for His sorrows and suffering (v. 3), taking upon Himself the struggles of the world (v. 4). Such affliction made it hard for anyone to view Him as favored by God like King David had been (1 Samuel 16:1). Instead, He seemed quite unfavored (v. 4).

Jesus' burdened life would culminate with an even more burdened death. God would place on Him all the weight of humanity's sin (v. 5). He would serve as the sacrificial lamb to be slaughtered (v. 7) in order to save the rest of the flock that had wandered in wrong directions (v. 6). Instead of mounting a throne, Jesus would mount a cross.

All of this is as un-king-like as it is un-Christmas-y. How is it reflective of the "arm of the LORD" (v. 1), in other words, the mighty workings of God, which Isaiah wanted people to recognize? The answer is conveyed by one phrase: "by his wounds we are healed" (v. 5), healed from all the wounds our sins inflict upon us. There is no mightier act God could accomplish.

When the Apostle John was given a glimpse into heaven, he wrote: "Then one of the elders said to me, 'Do not weep! See, the Lion of the tribe of Judah, the Root of David, has triumphed' ... Then I saw a Lamb, looking as if it had been slain, standing in the center of the throne … 'You are worthy,' the hosts of heaven sang to Him, 'because you were slain, and with your blood you purchased men for God from every tribe and language and people and nation. You have made them to be a kingdom'" (Revelation 5:5-6,9-10).

The One who created the kingdom is the King, and He is Jesus. He came to earth as an unrecognized King, as an unheralded and uncrowned King so that He could become an accepted King, accepted by individual hearts.

Prayer: I celebrate the coming of the One who may seem to be an unlikely choice for someone's allegiance. Though many in the world prefer to elevate someone or something else and though there's pressure on me to elevate anyone but Jesus, I bow to the king who mounted a cross for me rather than a throne for Himself.

Notes:

_____

_____

_____

_____

_____

_____

_____

_____

_____

_____

_____

Personal Prayer:

_____

_____

_____

_____

_____

_____

_____

_____

_____

_____

_____

_____

December 18

In the time of Herod king of Judea there was a priest named Zechariah... his wife Elizabeth was also a descendant of Aaron ... But they had no children, because Elizabeth was barren; and they were both well along in years.

Then an angel of the Lord appeared to him, standing at the right side of the altar of incense. When Zechariah saw him, he was startled and was gripped with fear. But the angel said to him: "Do not be afraid, Zechariah; your prayer has been heard. Your wife Elizabeth will bear you a son, and you are to give him the name John. He will be a joy and delight to you, and many will rejoice because of his birth, for he will be great in the sight of the Lord... Many of the people of Israel will he bring back to the Lord their God. And he will go on before the Lord in the spirit and power of Elijah... to make ready a people prepared for the Lord."

When his time of service was completed, he returned home. After this his wife Elizabeth became pregnant... "The Lord has done this for me," she said. "In these days he has shown his favor and taken away my disgrace among the people."

When it was time for Elizabeth to have her baby, she gave birth to a son. Her neighbors and relatives heard that the Lord had shown her great mercy, and they shared her joy.

On the eighth day they came to circumcise the child, and they were going to name him after his father Zechariah, but his mother spoke up and said, "No! He is to be called John."

The neighbors were all filled with awe, and throughout the hill country of Judea people were talking about all these things. Everyone who heard this wondered about it, asking, "What then is this child going to be?" For the Lord's hand was with him.

Luke 1:5-7,11-17,23-25,57-60,65-66 (from Luke 1:5-25,57-66)

Let the Miracles Begin

Throughout much of human history, when a couple was childless, it was considered the wife's shortcoming and viewed as a significant failure on her part. This is still the predominant thinking in many parts of the world. Even with modern science's capacity to pinpoint the problem more accurately, childless couples can suffer intense disappointment and heartache.

More than once in the Old Testament, we read about God reversing barrenness with the miraculous gift of a child. Notable cases include the birth of Isaac, Samson, and Samuel. In each instance, there were special words spoken to the husband or wife, making God's provision clear and underscoring that the child would have a unique calling on his life.

All of this was also the case for a New Testament couple, Zechariah and Elizabeth. There was barrenness (v. 7), stigma (v. 25), prayer for intervention (v. 13), and divine words about the role God had for their child (v. 15-17). It wasn't enough that Jesus' birth would be miraculous. Even the messenger who heralded His arrival would be the product of a miracle.

Perhaps after reading about several of these conception miracles, the impact lessens somewhat. Even so, there can be no doubt that the impact upon Zechariah and Elizabeth was enormous. This spiritually faithful couple (v. 6), had little hope of conceiving due to their age (v. 7). Then, in the midst of ordinary, everyday life (v. 8-10), God intervened with grace.

That's what their son's name "John" meant to everyone who heard it: "the LORD shows grace." His name was designated (v. 13) because his life's work was designated (v. 17). He would walk the countryside preparing people for the One "who came from the Father, full of grace" (John 1:14).

God marked this occasion with a visit by one of only two angels named in Scripture—Gabriel (v. 19). This is the angel who visited Daniel five hundred years earlier to reveal future events, the one who would announce the Messiah to Mary, and the one whose heavenly position is in the very presence of God (v. 19). He delivered "good news" (v. 19) to this couple, a precursor of the "good news" soon to be proclaimed to shepherds outside Bethlehem (Luke 2:10).

The joy of Zechariah and Elizabeth was joined by the joy of their neighbors and relatives (v. 57), just as Gabriel promised (v. 14-15). Imagine witnessing the miracles of Elizabeth's pregnancy, of the child's arrival, and of Zechariah's healing (v. 62-64). The people were filled with awe over such wonders (v. 65).

What no one could imagine, however, was the fulfillment of the rest of Gabriel's news. This son would minister in Elijah-like fashion (v. 17)—Elijah being an Old Testament prophet known for calling people to repentance. Like him, John would be rugged, fearless, powerful, and consumed by his mission (Matthew 3:1-10).

As Elijah was succeeded by the much greater Elisha (1 Kings 2:9-12), John would be succeeded by the much greater Jesus (Matthew 3:11). Likewise, Elizabeth's miracle of conception would be far exceeded by Mary's miracle of conception. John was given by God to bear the name of grace and identify its provider. Jesus would be given by God to make possible the overflow of grace to many (Romans 5:15). Let these miracles begin!

Prayer: I celebrate the coming of the One ushered into this world through miracles. As I consider the many miracles involved in Jesus' coming, I marvel that the Father would go to such lengths to usher the Son into my life. Those who still need Jesus are but a miracle away from His entrance. I pray for that miracle.

Notes:

_____
_____
_____
_____
_____
_____
_____
_____
_____
_____

Personal Prayer:

_____
_____
_____
_____
_____
_____
_____
_____
_____
_____
_____

December 19

In the sixth month, God sent the angel Gabriel to Nazareth, a town in Galilee, to a virgin pledged to be married to a man named Joseph, a descendant of David. The virgin's name was Mary. The angel went to her and said, "Greetings, you who are highly favored! The Lord is with you." Mary was greatly troubled at his words and wondered what kind of greeting this might be. But the angel said to her, "Do not be afraid, Mary, you have found favor with God. You will be with child and give birth to a son, and you are to give him the name Jesus. He will be great and will be called the Son of the Most High. The Lord God will give him the throne of his forefather David, and he will reign over the house of Jacob forever; his kingdom will never end." "How will this be," Mary asked the angel, "since I am a virgin?" The angel answered, "The Holy Spirit will come upon you, and the power of the Most Hight will overshadow you. So the holy one to be born will be called the Son of God. Even Elizabeth your relative is going to have a child in her old age, and she who was said to be barren is in her sixth month. For nothing is impossible with God." "I am the Lord's servant," Mary answered. "May it be to me as you have said." Then the angel left her.

Luke 1:26-38

Let the Grace Begin

There are miracles, and then there are miracles. Despite praying to an all-powerful God, we're prone to consciously or subconsciously envision tiers of difficulty, ranging from the unlikely to the impossible. Also, exercising faith for our own circumstances can be entirely different from viewing scriptural accounts of miracles as true. It's hard to believe in things we recognize to be impossible and harder still to believe in such things for ourselves.

Six months after Zechariah and Elizabeth conceived their son John, the angel Gabriel was dispatched from God's presence to an obscure village seventy miles north of Jerusalem (v. 26). The miracle he announced would far exceed the miracle of John's birth. With King David's throne nonexistent for more than five hundred years, the same length of time the nation was nonexistent, Gabriel announced both a king and a kingdom (v. 32-33). Furthermore, though engaged couples didn't even see each other between the betrothal ceremony and the wedding ceremony, Gabriel announced a conception (v. 31).

God was about to place these phenomenal miracles into the life of a lowly maiden. The reason is identified by Gabriel: Mary was a recipient of God's grace. That's the word translated "favor" in our English Bibles (v. 28,30). It's the same word found throughout the New Testament in reference to what provides our salvation—

God's "charis," grace, gift, undeserved favor. What John's name would proclaim, Mary's life was already experiencing.

Her child's name would be Jesus (v. 31), meaning "Jehovah is salvation." Unlike His forefather David who was promised a kingdom with specific geographic boundaries, this King would bring salvation and peace "to the nations" and would rule "from sea to sea," "to the ends of the earth" (Zechariah 9:9-10). Unlike the reign of King David, this King's reign would "never end" (v. 33).

As great as these promises must have sounded to Mary, her attention was on one thing—the absolute impossibility of a conception (v. 34). Her response wasn't unbelief as was the case with Zechariah (v. 18) but perplexity. What has been a tenet of faith in Christianity for over two thousand years—the virgin birth, God becoming man—wasn't even a concept for Mary. This miracle went far beyond the realm of impossibility. It was unimaginable.

However, Gabriel assured her that even the unfathomable is possible with God because nothing is impossible for Him (v. 37). Just as we might encourage each other, he urged her to use her belief in one miracle to help her wrap her heart around a much larger miracle (v. 36). Though we can't know everything that swirled within her, Mary's words of acceptance indicate her belief: "May it be to me as you have said" (v. 38).

The key words of this passage bring to mind another familiar passage of Scripture: "For it is by grace you have been saved, through faith" (Ephesians 2:8). Mary was given the opportunity to experience God's favor, God's grace. Through her belief, her faith in this grace, Jesus would enter her life and, thereby, enter our world—Jesus, whose very name means salvation. His first coming was by grace through faith, and He continues to come into individual lives in the very same way, even if it seems impossible.

Prayer: I celebrate the coming of the One brought into this world through grace. Just as God's greatest possible gift to a lowly maiden was the gift of His grace, I want to value His grace in my life as my greatest treasure. I praise God that the mightiest miracle in human history was a miracle of grace.

Notes:

Personal Prayer:

December 20

At that time Mary got ready and hurried to a town in the hill country of Judea, where she entered Zechariah's home and greeted Elizabeth. When Elizabeth heard Mary's greeting, the baby leaped in her womb, and Elizabeth was filled with the Holy Spirit. In a loud voice she exclaimed: "Blessed are you among women, and blessed is the child you will bear! But why am I so favored, that the mother of my Lord should come to me? As soon as the sound of your greeting reached my ears, the baby in my womb leaped for joy. Blessed is she who has believed that what the Lord has said to her will be accomplished."

Luke 1:39-45

Bolstering Belief

After the angel Gabriel informed Mary of Elizabeth's miraculous conception (v. 36), Mary seems to have left immediately to visit her relative Elizabeth. It was a distance of at least fifty miles, perhaps considerably further, depending upon Elizabeth's exact location in "the hill country of Judea" (v. 39). We may not know the specific relationship between the two women, but there's an interesting age difference with Elizabeth being in "old age" (v. 36) and Mary being a virgin of marrying age (v. 27).

What was in Mary's heart and mind as she traveled? It would have been a singularly joyful journey had Elizabeth's pregnancy been the only one of which Mary knew. However, she also must have been processing her own news of a coming birth. Whereas we have the luxury of reading history backwards, knowing all the positive endings that temper any challenges or struggles, she didn't have such an advantage. Gabriel had urged her to use Elizabeth's miracle to bolster her own belief (v. 35-37). Perhaps this visit was at least partially prompted by Mary's desire to gain spiritual strength for facing the daunting circumstances that lie ahead for her.

Oh, what a visit it was! When Mary entered the home and greeted Elizabeth, the baby in Elizabeth's womb "leaped" and Elizabeth was filled with the Holy Spirit (v. 40-41). Luke, the writer and a physician by vocation, presents the baby's movement as more than ordinary fetal activity; it was something spiritual because he identified it as a leap of joy (v. 44). The unborn child, who would one day herald Jesus' ministry and be the first to recognize Him as the Lamb of God (John 1:35-36) had a miraculous, in utero response to His coming.

And, just as Old Testament prophets were given a special anointing of God's Spirit, Elizabeth was anointed to prophesy regarding things she couldn't have known otherwise. Her son would be anointed from birth in a similar way (1:15) to be the powerful messenger who prepared the way for Jesus (Luke 7:24-27). For now, though, it was Elizabeth with a God-given message. In a loud voice, she proclaimed Mary's blessedness and the blessedness of her coming child (v. 42).

At this early stage, Elizabeth acknowledged Jesus' greatness (v. 43). He wasn't born yet, His full identity wasn't comprehended yet, and neither His teaching nor His miracles had started. Indeed, there were more questions than answers, as can be the case at various times in our own lives; but somehow in Elizabeth's spirit she knew to respond to Jesus with awe and to call Him "Lord."

Humanly speaking, Mary must have known her pregnancy risked the loss of her fiancé and the ruin of her reputation. Every aspect of her future was in jeopardy, including her very life as a perceived adulteress. Of all possible topics for a prophetic utterance at this moment, the one provided by God's Spirit specifically affirmed Mary's belief—her fundamental belief that God would do what He said He would do (v. 45).

One thing separated Mary from everything that threatened her. She had to believe in God's ability and faithfulness to do what He said He would do. How remarkable to watch God provide an angel, a leaping unborn child, a Spirit-filled woman, and a prophetic pronouncement—all to bolster Mary's belief.

Prayer: I celebrate the coming of the One worthy of my belief. When believing is especially challenging because the future is bombarded with threats of uncertainty and peril, I ask for help believing. And, I ask for help recognizing God's personal assurances that He'll be faithful to do everything He says He'll do.

Notes:

_____

_____

_____

_____

_____

_____

_____

_____

_____

Personal Prayer:

_____

_____

_____

_____

_____

_____

_____

_____

_____

_____

December 21

And Mary said, "My soul glorifies the Lord and my spirit rejoices in God my Savior, for he has been mindful of the humble state of his servant. From now on all generations will call me blessed, for the Mighty One has done great things for me—holy is his name. His mercy extends to those who fear him, from generation to generation. He has performed mighty deeds with his arm; he has scattered those who are proud in their inmost thoughts. He has brought down rulers from their thrones but has lifted up the humble. He has filled the hungry with good things but has sent the rich away empty. He has helped his servant Israel, remembering to be merciful to Abraham and his descendants forever, even as he said to our fathers."

Luke 1:46-55

Let the Rejoicing Begin

There's no better evidence of Mary's belief in God's trustworthiness than the words to what's often called the "Magnificat" or "Mary's Song." After she had received a prophetic blessing from her relative Elizabeth, affirming her faith in God doing what He said He would do (v. 45), Mary broke into these words. Whether she sang them or shouted them or danced them or merely spoke them, there's no psalm in all of Scripture that overflows with more elegance or truth.

It's important to remember that none of Mary's potentially problematic circumstances had changed one bit. What her words indicate is the placing of her focus upon God rather than upon her circumstances. Only He is all-loving, all-knowing, all-powerful, everywhere present, and completely outside the confines of time. When we step out of our earthly perspective into God's perspective, our concerns rest in the safety of His unstoppable plan of redemption for us. This is the plan that matters because it's the plan that will be victorious and eternal.

From the depths of Mary's being, from what can only be labeled her "soul" or "spirit" (v. 47), she began to magnify ("magnificat" in Latin) God. Put simply, she began praising Him, but it's helpful to realize that praising God consists of magnifying or making God large with our words. And, what a perfect starting point for Mary's praise—rejoicing over God being her Savior (v. 47).

Her reference to being called "blessed" (enjoying well-being) for generations to come (v. 48) centers all the attention on God. Indeed, the only descriptor Mary gives of herself refers to her lowly status (v. 48). It's God who is credited with being mindful of her (v. 48), being the Mighty One, and doing great things for her (v. 49). It is His name, hence, His character that's said to be holy (v. 49).

Mary identifies the amazing counterbalance of God's mercy (v. 50) and might (v. 51). How desperately all of us need Him to exercise both of these traits on our behalf. Yet, how rarely earthly leaders emulate the combination. Instead, they think their might relieves them of the responsibility to exercise mercy. Mary cites multiple instances of God reversing the ways of mankind with this remarkable twosome (v. 51-53).

There's no way to know if Mary realized she was also describing the One she would name Jesus, but she certainly was. His teaching, particularly conveyed by the Sermon on the Mount (Matthew 5-7), gives example after example of earthly priorities being turned upside down by the values of God's kingdom, the kingdom Jesus came to establish. The proud (v. 51), the powerful (v. 52), and the rich (v. 53) are displaced in favor of those who are humble (v. 52) and hungry (v. 53).

Again Mary mentions God's mercy and the faithful demonstration of it throughout Israel's history (v. 54).

With a focus fixed upon a faithful God, she was about to give birth to the One who would be the greatest display of His faithfulness, the One who fulfills every promise made to Abraham and his descendants (v. 55), the One who keeps a dawn-of-creation promise to bless the entire world (Genesis 12:1-3). Even with perplexing circumstances swirling about, God's faithfulness is cause for rejoicing!

Prayer: I celebrate the coming of the One who brings rejoicing to my heart because of His provision of redemption. I'm amazed that He's mindful of me. I welcome the establishing of His kingdom in my life with its reversal of earthly priorities and its care for the humble. I'm thrilled to call him Savior.

Notes:

___

Personal Prayer:

___

December 22

This is how the birth of Jesus Christ came about: His mother Mary was pledged to be married to Joseph, but before they came together, she was found to be with child through the Holy Spirit. Because Joseph her husband was a righteous man and did not want to expose her to public disgrace, he had in mind to divorce her quietly. But after he had considered this, an angel of the Lord appeared to him in a dream and said, "Joseph son of David, do not be afraid to take Mary home as your wife, because what is conceived in her is from the Holy Spirit. She will give birth to a son, and you are to give him the name Jesus, because he will save his people from their sins." All this took place to fulfill what the Lord had said through the prophet: "The virgin will be with child and will give birth to a son, and they will call him Immanuel—which means, God with us." When Joseph woke up, he did what the angel of the Lord had commanded him and took Mary home as his wife. But he had no union with her until she gave birth to a son. And he gave him the name Jesus.

Matthew 1:18-25

There's Been a Change of Plans

A completely different life could have flowed out of the genealogy summarized in Matthew 1:2-16. In fact, Joseph's plan for his life was already in place when God's plan for him was revealed. Joseph knew who he was, traceable all the way back to his forefather Abraham and very important to any first-century Jewish man. However, only God could orchestrate who he was meant to be.

The change of plans unfolded while Joseph was in between betrothal (v. 18) and marriage (v. 24), a period that typically lasted a year. Though an engaged couple lived apart and were not to see each other, the arrangement was as binding as marriage. This being the case, Joseph was already referred to as Mary's husband (v. 19). Their pledge could only be broken by divorce, and any unfaithfulness was viewed as adultery.

The genealogy recorded by Matthew presents Joseph as the legal heir to the throne of David (v. 2-16). This mattered very little, however, since the throne had been vacated for more than five hundred years due to there being no nation for a king to rule. Instead, Joseph worked as a carpenter (Matthew 13:55) in the province of Galilee, in the village of Nazareth (Luke 2:4), a town with no regard in the eyes of his people (John 1:46).

These components of Joseph's life may or may not seem like much to us, but they were reflective of his day and, most importantly, they comprised the path he expected his life to follow. Then, suddenly and drastically, everything changed. Mary was pregnant (v. 18), even though Joseph had not yet been intimate with her (v. 18). Despite the couple's chastity, Joseph knew what everyone would conclude about the pregnancy.

In addition to the emotional impact of the news, a spiritual wrestling must have ensued because Joseph was "a righteous man" (v. 19), an expression used of those who were zealous to obey Old Testament law. To marry his fiancé would make him appear guilty of sexual immorality. To renounce her by public divorce, ridding himself of all blame, would inflict enormous shame upon her.

As Joseph considered the best solution for coping with his world being turned upside down (v. 19), God sent a message to him (v. 20). An angel greeted him as "Joseph son of David" (v. 20). Whether or not he viewed himself as titled, God was about to use the legal heir to David's throne to become the legal father of the One who would sit on that throne forever.

No Jewish woman could have envisioned a greater honor than to bear the Messiah. Similarly, the highest hope of any Jewish man was to see Israel's throne reestablished. Both miracles would be accomplished through Mary and Joseph. So, what's not to embrace about such a wonderful change of plans?

From Joseph's human perspective, all the normalcy he had anticipated was gone. Every day of his life, he would have to believe in the greatest miracle the world has ever experienced (v. 20). Though it fulfilled a familiar Old Testament prophecy (v. 23; Isaiah 7:14), it was nonetheless something people would find hard to believe. Even decades later, whispers about Jesus' birth persisted (John 8:41).

God's plan for Joseph was anchored in Joseph's true identity as David's descendant. In turn, it was to Joseph that the angel announced the child's true identity. He would "save his people from their sins" (v. 21). And, even more amazing, He would be recognized as "Immanuel," meaning "God with us" (v. 23).

No matter how skillful Joseph may have been on his carpenter's bench, nothing would ever compare with the special life God had crafted for him to live.

Prayer: I celebrate the coming of the One who exchanges my lesser plans for His greater plans. Despite the risks inherent in change, I want to remain ever pliable in the hands of the One who not only knows who I am but also knows who I'm meant to be in God's unfolding, eternal plan.

Notes:

_____
_____
_____
_____
_____
_____
_____
_____
_____

Personal Prayer:

_____
_____
_____
_____
_____
_____
_____
_____
_____
_____
_____

December 23

In those days Caesar Augustus issued a decree that a census should be taken of the entire Roman world. (This was the first census that took place while Quirinius was governor of Syria.) And everyone went to his own town to register. So Joseph also went up from the town of Nazareth in Galilee to Judea, to Bethlehem the town of David, because he belonged to the house and line of David. He went there to register with Mary, who was pledged to be married to him and was expecting a child. While they were there, the time came for the baby to be born, and she gave birth to her firstborn, a son. She wrapped him in cloths and placed him in a manger, because there was no room for them in the inn.

Luke 2:1-7

What Exactly Just Happened?

How simply and succinctly the event of all time is recorded. Yet, with the delicate style of a literary masterpiece, themes are placed before the reader that are clearly discernible. Hence, we read how Jesus was born into politics, prophecy, and poverty.

The prominence of politics in Jesus' day had to do with the Roman Empire, one of the greatest kingdoms the world has ever known. Octavian was its first emperor. To his family name of Caesar, the Roman Senate added the title of Augustus, meaning "exalted." Thus, Octavian became Caesar Augustus. His military and political abilities were extraordinary, and his forty-year reign was marked by phenomenal authority and achievement.

A census decree (v. 1) was nothing unusual. It was used for taxation purposes and, in favorable locations, to identify eligible candidates for military service. It would have been the responsibility of lower-level rulers throughout the empire, such as Quirinius (v. 2), to conduct the count within their own region. As governor of the province of Syria, which stretched along the eastern side of the Mediterranean Sea, including the territories of Galilee and Judea, Quirinius' approach was to have the heads of households register in their ancestral homes (v. 3).

This means an emperor's decree coupled with a regional governor's implementation put Jesus in

Bethlehem at the time of His birth. Or, did it? Seven hundred years earlier, when Rome was nothing but a modest settlement on a faraway continent, an Old Testament prophet announced: "But you, Bethlehem Ephrathah, though you are small among the clans of Judah, out of you will come for me one who will be ruler over Israel" (Micah 5:2).

Joseph's journey from his residence in Nazareth to Bethlehem (v. 4) certainly appeared to be caused by the politics of a census. More importantly, though, prophecy launched the trip for entirely other reasons. Bethlehem was the lowly, unlikely place from which David was chosen by God a thousand years earlier to be king of Israel (1 Samuel 16). Joseph and Mary were in the lineage of David's dynasty (v. 4). Another seven-hundred-year-old prophecy said of them, "The virgin will be with child and will give birth to a son, and will call him Immanuel" (Isaiah 7:14). This offspring of David would be born in the same lowly, unlikely town of Bethlehem, just as the prophet Micah foretold.

In the juxtaposing of politics and prophecy, there was a sovereignty controlling the place of Jesus' birth, but it was God and not Caesar Augustus. Similarly, the circumstances of Jesus' birth were divinely controlled.

It wasn't necessary for Mary to accompany Joseph (v. 5) on the three-day trip from Galilee "up" into the hill country of Judea (v. 4). Whatever the reason, perhaps Joseph deciding it was unwise or unkind to leave her to the talk of their hometown, the away-from-home birth that followed Mary's journey (v. 6-7) made their poverty all the more pronounced. In a village crowded with census travelers, they managed no better accommodations than sheltering themselves where a feeding trough served as a cradle (v. 7).

Questionable judgment on their part? To the contrary, the One who would minister to the poor would be conspicuously poor Himself. He would endure physical poverty to give us spiritual riches (2 Corinthians 8:9). That's who was placed by God in a manger in Bethlehem in the midst of politics and prophecy.

Prayer: I celebrate the coming of the One who has born in Bethlehem as a result of all things earthly yielding to all things spiritual. With God's ability to control thousands of years of details, I entrust the details of my life to His sovereignty, and I entrust the poverty of my life to His rich provisions.

Notes:

_____

_____

_____

_____

_____

_____

_____

_____

_____

_____

_____

Personal Prayer:

_____

_____

_____

_____

_____

_____

_____

_____

_____

_____

_____

_____

December 24

And there were shepherds living out in the fields at night. An angel of the Lord appeared to them and the glory of the Lord shone around them, and they were terrified. But the angel said to them, "Do not be afraid. I bring you good news of great joy that will be for all the people. Today in the town of David a Savior has been born to you; he is Christ the Lord. This will be a sign to you: You will find a baby wrapped in cloths and lying in a manger." Suddenly a great company of the heavenly host appeared with the angel, praising God and saying, "Glory to God in the highest, and on earth peace to men on whom his favor rests."

Luke 2:8-14

Look Who Received an Invitation

The Son of God was born! Who would be first to receive the news? Jerusalem was only five miles away, providing an array of religious dignitaries as well as business moguls and government officials. Who would heaven prioritize to learn about Jesus' coming?

Unexpectedly, it was to shepherds during their night watch (v. 8) that an angel appeared and set the landscape aglow with heavenly glory (v. 9). The shepherds' initial reaction of fear was understandable (v. 9), but the angel immediately identified the message as "good news of great joy" (v. 10). Still, why were they the recipients of the news?

The hillside scene strikes us as pleasantly quaint; but, in the first century, shepherds were of low social rank and were viewed as having questionable integrity. Aspects of their work rendered them continually ceremonially unclean, something that mattered a great deal. Their flocks had to be guarded against predatory animals and thieves by day and night, making their outdoor life even more arduous.

It's likely King David grazed his flocks in the very same fields during his shepherd years. It was his successor whose birth the angel announced. This progeny would be "the good shepherd" of His flock of human souls (John 10:14), and He would ascend to David's throne to reign forever (Luke 1:32-33).

Herdsmen who used the pastures near Jerusalem are thought to have provided the temple's sacrificial animals. To them the angel announced that a "Savior" was born (v. 11). He is "Christ" (v. 11), the Greek equivalent of the Hebrew word "Messiah," meaning "anointed one." He is also "Lord" (v. 11), a designation for God Himself. Heaven knew that God the Son was the anointed one, anointed to be the perfect sacrifice that would end all sacrifices and thereby provide our Savior (John 1:29).

So, it was to fellow shepherds that the lowly one, the good shepherd, the sacrificial lamb was announced. Who better to recognize Jesus than those who knew so much about who He was sent to be? It's true that they would have expected to be saved from their poverty, sickness, political oppression, and other earthly ills. What made the news "good news of great joy" (v. 10) was that He would be their Savior from sin, the greatest ill of all.

A thousand years earlier, the shepherd-king David wrote, "The heavens declare the glory of God" (Psalm 19:1); but what David saw in the skies of his day didn't compare to what these shepherds witnessed. An army of heavenly beings suddenly appeared, praising God. Their words "Glory to God in the highest" (v. 14) in Latin comprise the chorus of "Hark the Herald Angels Sing": "Gloria in Excelsis Deo!"

The "great company of the heavenly host" (v. 13) announced a blessing of peace upon those who have

God's favor (v. 14), in other words, upon those who please God by exercising faith in Him. Such individuals experience the Hebrew concept of peace—well-being within their souls.

It's hard to imagine what it was like to see the sky explode with angels and praises. All of it was focused on "a baby wrapped in cloths and lying in a manger" (v. 12). The grandeur of heaven announced to lowly shepherds that it would be out of lowliness (v. 12) that God would accomplish the grandeur of being the Savior "for all the people" (v. 10). Glory to God in the highest!

Prayer: I celebrate the coming of the One who was announced by heaven to lowly, unclean, and perhaps unscrupulous shepherds because they needed Him and because they would recognize Him. May my own need for Him be coupled with an increased capacity to recognize Him as my Savior and the Savior of the world.

Notes:

_____

_____

_____

_____

_____

_____

_____

_____

_____

_____

Personal Prayer:

_____

_____

_____

_____

_____

_____

_____

_____

_____

_____

_____

_____

December 25

When the angels had left them and gone into heaven, the shepherds said to one another, "Let's go to Bethlehem and see this thing that has happened, which the Lord has told us about." They hurried off and found Mary and Joseph, and the baby, who was lying in the manger. When they had seen him, they spread the word concerning what had been told them about this child, and all who heard it were amazed at what the shepherds said to them. But Mary treasured up all these things and pondered them in her heart. The shepherds returned, glorifying and praising God for all the things they had heard and seen, which were just as they had been told.

Luke 2:15-20

Check the Gift Tag

How appropriate that this Christmas Day passage has everything to do with how we receive the gift of Jesus' coming.

The shepherds weren't commanded or instructed to visit Jesus. They were invited by way of the information provided in the angel's message (v. 11-12). It was their desire to locate Jesus because they realized they had just heard from God (v. 15). Not all messages from God come with dazzling light, armies of angels, and choruses of praise; but all messages from God invite a response.

There's a suggestion of urgency in the Greek wording of the shepherds' comments to each other (v. 15). This, coupled with the fact that they "hurried off" (v. 16), evidently while it was still nighttime, indicates their excitement. They believed the angel that the Messiah was born. Their words weren't "see if this thing has happened" but "see this thing that has happened" (v. 15). Believing that the Anointed One had come, they hurried to make His coming their personal experience.

Whether it was the small size of Bethlehem, the availability of perhaps only one inn (v. 7), or the rarity of an expectant couple being housed in a stable; the shepherds "found Mary and Joseph, and the baby" (v. 16). Compelling as the angelic visitation must have been, having the angel's words confirmed to be true must have had its own special impact upon each shepherd.

Their enthusiasm extended beyond seeing Jesus. They began spreading the word about His identity (v. 17). Though not capable of any scholarly presentation, they were fully capable of sharing the simple testimony of common men. It can be assumed that the social sphere of herdsmen was limited to other commoners. That's who received the ministry of these first evangelists, and, later, it's who would receive Jesus' ministry.

All who heard the shepherds' news marveled (v. 18). They were amazed, astonished. The same word would often be used in people's reactions to Jesus' teaching and miracles. It's a positive response but sometimes unfinished or short-lived. Many people who marveled would be among those who left Jesus once He identified Himself more fully (John 6:66).

In contrast to being amazed, the text says, "But Mary … treasured … and pondered … in her heart" (v. 19). The shepherds would have told her and Joseph about the angel's words and the display of angelic praise that filled the sky. This report would have been in addition to what the couple had already experienced with angelic appearances, plus the birth itself. This was an enormous amount to process.

It's not that Mary and Joseph didn't experience amazement. The very same word "marveled" is used for them when they visit the temple (v. 33) and hear even more about the child Jesus. The point is, sometimes the best place for astonishing things is in the safety of our hearts, there to treasure and ponder.

The rest of the shepherds' responses to Jesus' coming reflect the rejoicing of Mary that's recorded earlier (Luke 1:46-55). They returned to their work and their lives "glorifying and praising God for all the things they had heard and seen" (v. 20). A gift had been given, and they recognized who gave it and to whom it was given.

> Prayer: I celebrate the coming of the One who is God's gift to me. Whether I've known Jesus for a day or a lifetime, I pray for a continued awareness that He is a priceless gift from God. I pray for the amazement and enthusiasm of the shepherds, and I pray for the quiet pondering of Mary.

Notes:

Personal Prayer:

December 26

On the eighth day, when it was time to circumcise him, he was named Jesus, the name the angel had given him before he had been conceived. When the time of their purification according to the Law of Moses had been completed, Joseph and Mary took him to Jerusalem to present him to the Lord (as it is written in the Law of the Lord, "Every firstborn male is to be consecrated to the Lord") and to offer a sacrifice in keeping with what is said in the Law of the Lord: "a pair of doves or two young pigeons."

Luke 2:21-24

One Step at a Time

It's easy to lose sight of what Joseph and Mary faced. True, both had experienced a heavenly visitation. Also, there was the miracle child of Zechariah and Elizabeth, the encouraging encounter between Mary and Elizabeth, and the visit of shepherds who told about a whole sky full of angels. Still, there would have been the "everydayness" that followed Jesus' birth as well as thoughts of returning home where challenging reactions awaited them.

How did this chosen couple press into their God-given assignment? Quite simply, they obeyed God's Word. Much of the Law given to Moses for Israel consisted of symbolic ceremonial practices meant to prepare people to recognize their sin, acknowledge their need for redemption, and accept God's provision of a Savior. Once Jesus stepped fully and perfectly into these ceremonies, He became the fulfillment of the Law. With baby Jesus in their arms, Joseph and Mary obeyed the ceremonial components of the Law just as faithfully as if there were nothing unusual about them or their child.

The Old Testament specified that a woman was considered ceremonially unclean for seven days after giving birth to a son (Leviticus 12:1-2). This had to do with the discharge of bodily fluids for women or men (Leviticus 15) and the use of it as an object lesson to teach about spiritual impurity. On the eighth day after birth, a baby boy was to be circumcised (Leviticus 12:3). Joseph and Mary dutifully obeyed this command (v. 21).

In addition to adhering to the Law's stipulation about circumcision, the couple also obeyed what an angel had specified to them. Joseph's angelic visitation was in a dream (Matthew 1:18-25); whereas, Mary's was in person (Luke 1:26-38). The messages they received shared three things in common: Mary would conceive of the Holy Spirit, she would give birth to a son, and they were to name Him "Jesus." Because names designated character, it was important for God's Son to bear the name meaning "Jehovah is salvation."

The Old Testament further specified that a woman giving birth to a son remained ceremonially unclean for an additional thirty-three days (Leviticus 12:4), totaling forty days. During the entirety of this time, she wasn't to enter the temple. After these forty days, she was to present herself to the priest for purification, bringing either a lamb and a pigeon (or a dove) as sacrifices or, if she were poor, two pigeons (or two doves) (Leviticus 12:6-8).

We read of Joseph and Mary complying with this requirement and see from the text that they offered the sacrifice of the poor, evidently unable to afford a lamb (v. 24). How striking that they had in their arms the Lamb of God, who was priceless—valuable enough to atone for the sins of the whole world.

The couple used their temple visit to present or dedicate Jesus (v. 22-23), also in obedience to the Law.

Each firstborn son was considered God's special possession for service in the priesthood (Exodus 13:1-2,11-16). This responsibility was absolved and, instead, carried out by the descendants of Levi (Number 3:11-13) upon paying a five-shekel redemption price (Numbers 18:15-16), which Joseph and Mary did (v. 27).

Whether their hearts were filled with ecstasy, perplexity, concern, or a combination of every possible emotion, Joseph and Mary are portrayed by Scripture as simply doing what they knew to be the right things to do.

Prayer: I celebrate the coming of the One who causes me to be obedient to God's Word. Amidst the everydayness of my life, I want to be obedient. Amidst all concerns that arise, I want to be obedient. When I know nothing else to do, I want to do what I know to be the right things to do.

Notes:

___

Personal Prayer:

___

December 27

Now there was a man in Jerusalem called Simeon, who was righteous and devout. He was waiting for the consolation of Israel, and the Holy Spirit was upon him. It had been revealed to him by the Holy Spirit that he would not die before he had seen the Lord's Christ. Moved by the Spirit, he went into the temple courts. When the parents brought in the child Jesus to do for him what the custom of the Law required, Simeon took him in his arms and praised God saying: "Sovereign Lord, as you have promised, you now dismiss your servant in peace. For my eyes have seen your salvation, which you have prepared in the sight of all people, a light for revelation to the Gentiles and for glory to your people Israel." The child's father and mother marveled at what was said about him. Then Simeon blessed them and said to Mary, his mother: "This child is destined to cause the falling and rising of many in Israel, and to be a sign that will be spoken against, so that the thoughts of many hearts will be revealed. And a sword will pierce your own soul too." There was also a prophetess, Anna, the daughter of Phanuel, of the tribe of Asher. She was very old; she had lived with her husband seven years after her marriage, and then was a widow until she was eighty-four. She never left the temple but worshiped night and day, fasting and praying. Coming up to them at that very moment, she gave thanks to God and spoke about the child to all who were looking forward to the redemption of Jerusalem.

Luke 2:25-38

Being in the Know

God had quite a reception awaiting Joseph and Mary when they made their appearance at the temple. They were familiar with Old Testament prophets being anointed by God's Spirit to proclaim messages to Israel. However, there hadn't been a prophet for four hundred years and probably no special anointing of the Spirit for any large-scale purpose during the same period—not until Elizabeth's miracle baby leaped in her womb and she was filled with the Holy Spirit (Luke 1:41).

The writer Luke is careful to identify the credentials of Simeon and Anna, so as to give their utterances full authority. Simeon was recognized as "righteous and devout" (v. 25), the Holy Spirit rested upon him (v. 25), he was committed to awaiting God's intervention for Israel (v. 25), and he had God's assurance of witnessing the Messiah's coming (v. 26). With perfect timing orchestrated by God's Spirit, he entered the exterior courts of the temple just as Joseph and Mary were there (v. 27).

Anna is said to be a prophetess (v. 36), in other words, a female prophet. Old Testament prophets held a higher ranking than priests in various ways, including speaking for God to the people as opposed to priests who spoke for the people to God. Anna's presence in the temple was so constant that she was referred to as never leaving (v. 37). Priests were on duty according to a rotating schedule, but she "worshiped day and night, fasting and praying" (v. 37). The timing of her encounter with Joseph and Mary sounds as providential as that of Simeon (v. 38).

It was by God's Spirit that these two seekers of truth recognized Jesus. There were no other signals. In fact, the lowliness of the couple would have suggested the opposite of presenting the Messiah. But God, in His goodness and generosity, chose to let two faithful individuals see the Christ and let Simeon hold Him in his arms (v. 28).

The honor and joy were sufficient enough for Simeon to need nothing else in life (v. 29). He was witnessing God's salvation (v. 30), prepared for all people (v. 31). With spiritual insight, he saw in Jesus a light that would be a revelation for all the Gentiles of the world and would be glory for Israel (v. 32) because the Savior had come through them.

Jesus' parents (Joseph being His legal father) "marveled" at Simeon's words (v. 33), perhaps that he could know such things or that Jesus' ministry would extend to Gentiles. Simeon's blessing upon the couple, however, included heart-wrenching words for Mary, warning her of the personal pain she would experience watching Jesus fulfill His calling. It would be like a large sword piercing not only Jesus' heart but her heart also (v. 35).

Depending upon acceptance or rejection of the salvation Simeon cradled in his arms, countrymen would rise or fall (v. 34), revealing what was in their hearts toward Jesus (v. 35). He would be a sign pointing to God, but many would speak against the sign (v. 32). To all of this Anna added her thanks to God for Jesus, and she began telling others of Him (v. 38).

From a first-century temple courtyard to the individual lives of people today, certain things remain the same, including the work of God's Spirit revealing Jesus to be God's salvation. As Simeon and Anna experienced, we still experience—the "Spirit of truth" testifies to us about Jesus (John 15:26).

> Prayer: I celebrate the coming of the One who is the fulfillment of God's plan of redemption. As a seeker of truth, may I see past Jesus' lowliness and recognize His greatness. May my heart be fully open to every truth about Him that the Spirit reveals to me. And, then, may I testify to others about His salvation.

Notes:

Personal Prayer:

December 28

After Jesus was born in Bethlehem in Judea, during the time of King Herod, Magi from the east came to Jerusalem and asked, "Where is the one who has been born king of the Jews? We saw his star in the east and have come to worship him." When King Herod heard this he was disturbed, and all Jerusalem with him. When he had called together all the people's chief priests and teachers of the law, he asked them where the Christ was to be born. "In Bethlehem in Judea," they replied, "for this is what the prophet has written: 'But you, Bethlehem, in the land of Judah, are by no means least among the rulers of Judah; for out of you will come a ruler who will be the shepherd of my people Israel.'"

Matthew 2:1-6

Look Who Else Was Invited

With each of the Gospels being distinct in what its author includes and excludes, following the events of Luke 2:25-38, Matthew inserts a component of Jesus' coming that's unique to his account. It's an occurrence that's placed into nativity scenes and recounted by children so routinely as to smooth off some of its sharp, surprising edges.

Herod the Great (v. 1), distinguished from lesser members of the Herod family dynasty, was appointed by the Roman Senate to rule over the Jews of Palestine. His 37-year reign was marked by political astuteness, extensive building projects, and ruthlessness. During his later years, his jealousy frequently escalated into extreme paranoia. He killed his wife, three of his sons, various other relatives, and scores of perceived rivals in repeated efforts to guard his throne from the slightest threat.

It was during King Herod's reign that King Jesus was born, only five miles away. Evidently, Herod hadn't heard about the shepherds' angelic visitation in the fields near Bethlehem or Simeon's and Anna's recognition of the baby in Jerusalem's temple. He was alerted, however, when foreigners arrived, looking for a recently born "king of the Jews" (v. 2-3).

Who these Magi were is impossible to say. From its original reference to a priestly caste in Persia hundreds of years earlier, the term "Magi" evolved into a loose designation for anyone practicing dream interpretation, magic arts, and/or astrology. Magi were located in many locations east of Jerusalem (v. 1), including Arabia and Babylon. Found among them were sincere truth seekers, rogue charlatans, and everything in between.

There are additional mysteries about this passage. For example, which "star" the Magi saw (v. 2) is unknown. There are various theories about converging planets, novas and supernovas (star explosions), and comets—any of which could have presented a star-like appearance. If the phenomenon was natural, it was out of the ordinary enough to be highly significant; yet it may have been entirely supernatural.

How the Magi associated the star with a kingly birth is also unknown. There was a sizable Jewish settlement in Babylon that could have acquainted them with a Messianic prophecy suggesting the connection (Numbers 24:17). Or, this knowledge, like the star itself, could have been supernaturally revealed to them.

The Magi aren't said to be three in number, aren't said to be kings in any way, aren't even said to have followed a moving star from their origin in the east. Their journey may have been a matter of looking for the King of the Jews in what had been the Jews' capital city, Jerusalem. Indeed, it's not explanations that Matthew presents but oddities.

First, there's the disparity between two kings. One seems to be exceedingly powerful but is nothing more than an undeserving political appointee. The other seems unrecognized and uncrowned, but His right to the throne is by virtue of birth. Indeed, Jesus wasn't born to be king; He was "born king" (v. 2).

Second, pagan diviners, whose sin is denounced by Scripture (Isaiah 47:12-15), were chosen by God to witness Jesus' coming… because God knew how rightly they would respond. When their seeking of Jesus disturbed Herod and Herod's potential for cruelty disturbed all of Jerusalem (v. 3), Jewish chief priests and other Old Testament experts were called together to provide information (v. 4). Yes, the religious elite knew much about the Messiah's birth (v. 5-6), but their disinterest contrasts sharply with the eager-to-worship Magi.

Whether lowly shepherds or sinful astrologers, God surprises us with His invitation list to King Jesus' coming; but these individuals' responses to God's invitation didn't surprise Him at all.

Prayer: I celebrate the coming of the One whose focus is more on a sinner's response than a sinner's background. I ask for the same focus so that I never view someone as undeserving of Jesus whose response to Him would put seasoned religious people to shame. I want to learn from abject pagans how to value Jesus.

Notes:

_____

_____

_____

_____

_____

_____

_____

_____

_____

_____

Personal Prayer:

_____

_____

_____

_____

_____

_____

_____

_____

_____

_____

_____

December 29

Then Herod called the Magi secretly and found out from them the exact time the star had appeared. He sent them to Bethlehem and said, "Go and make a careful search for the child. As soon as you find him, report to me, so that I too may go and worship him." After they had heard the king, they went on their way, and the star they had seen in the east went ahead of them until it stopped over the place where the child was. When they saw the star, they were overjoyed. On coming to the house, they saw the child with his mother Mary, and they bowed down and worshiped him. Then they opened their treasures and presented him with gifts of gold and of incense and of myrrh. And having been warned in a dream not to go back to Herod, they returned to their country by another route.

Matthew 2:7-12

You're Not the Boss of Me

We can only begin to imagine the kowtowing that Herod the Great enjoyed on a regular basis. Other than a few things that had to be granted by a few individuals ranked higher than he in the Roman Empire, his every command would have been obeyed because this despot thought nothing of ordering someone's death. Within his sphere of rule, he was the unchallenged authority over everyone and everything.

With Jesus' birth location gained from the religious officials (v. 4-6), Herod ordered an appearance by the Magi to determine an estimate of the birth date according to the star's initial appearance (v. 7). He took the precaution of conducting this session in secret, though it doesn't seem that the Magi were suspicious of him. Their inclination was to worship the special child, so it was only natural for them to believe Herod wished to do likewise, just as he claimed (v. 8).

In truth, Herod's intentions were the opposite. The Jews expected the Roman Empire's control over Palestine, which was Herod's domain, to be overthrown by a descendant of King David. Herod would have known this because insurgents were active and persistent enough for him to learn of these expectations. It's possible he viewed his greatest threat to be a return of David's Dynasty. There's no doubt that Herod planned to execute the very child the Magi planned to worship.

He would use the Magi to do the legwork of scouring Bethlehem for the aspiring king. What better guise than foreigners who wished to pay homage? Then, once they reported their findings to him (v. 8), he would have the child killed and probably have the Magi killed as well for daring to think there was any king over the region but him.

The text reads as if the star reappeared (v. 10), suggesting the Magi saw it from their home in the east but hadn't followed it to Jerusalem. Understandably, seeing it again caused great joy (v. 10). The length of their journey, likely two years (v. 16), would have been a lengthy lapse to go without seeing that promising light. Herod may have directed them to Bethlehem (v. 8), but it was the star that directed them to Jesus' exact location (v. 9) in some type of "house" (v. 11) into which the family had moved. Perhaps Joseph had found work in his carpentry trade (Matthew 13:55).

There was no appearance of royalty about Jesus, but the Magi "bowed down and worshiped him" (v. 11). It wasn't the knowledgeable religious hierarchy honoring David's offspring in David's town. It was foreigners, pagans. But it was because they sought the truth. They lavished Jesus with expensive gifts, including two tree resins, one of which was used as aromatic incense and the other for perfume and burials.

Scholars note that gold symbolizes Jesus' royalty, incense His divinity, and myrrh His suffering and death. To the Magi, the gifts were simply an extravagant expression of their regard for the King. For Joseph and Mary, the treasures probably supplied funding for their family during its unexpected travels.

We're not at all surprised that God made sure the men who were invited to witness Jesus' coming returned to their homes safely (v. 12). And, we're not at all surprised that, for God, Herod the Great was no threat whatsoever.

Prayer: I celebrate the coming of the One whose mission cannot be stopped. No matter who or what attempts to bully me, even when I don't realize there's a bully targeting me, I'm going to worship Jesus. I'm going to offer Him gifts of value from my life in response to who He is.

Notes:

___

Personal Prayer:

December 30

When they had gone, an angel of the Lord appeared to Joseph in a dream. "Get up," he said, "take the child and his mother and escape to Egypt. Stay there until I tell you, for Herod is going to search for the child to kill him." So he got up, took the child and his mother during the night and left for Egypt, where he stayed until the death of Herod. And so was fulfilled what the Lord had said through the prophet: "Out of Egypt I called my son." When Herod realized that he had been outwitted by the Magi, he was furious, and he gave orders to kill all the boys in Bethlehem and its vicinity who were two years old and under, in accordance with the time he had learned from the Magi. Then what was said through the prophet Jeremiah was fulfilled: "A voice is heard in Ramah, weeping and great mourning, Rachel weeping for her children and refusing to be comforted, because they are no more."

Matthew 2:13-18

Sin, Sorrow, and Salvation

With multiple appearances of angels involved in the coming of Jesus, both in person and in dreams, it's easy for yet another appearance (v. 13) to strike us as somewhat routine. For Joseph, however, there was nothing routine about a heavenly warning of Jesus' life being in jeopardy at the hands of Herod (v. 13). Herdsmen and foreigners managed to locate them; it's likely the king and his armies would have no difficulty.

The narrative moves quickly. The Magi were directed by the star, indicating they traveled the five miles from Herod in Jerusalem to the family in Bethlehem by night (v. 9). It may have been when Joseph fell asleep the same night that he had the dream. He seems to have left immediately (v. 14). It was at least a hundred miles to Egypt's closest border, safely out of Herod's jurisdiction but a long and arduous journey.

For Joseph to tackle such a trip, he must have believed the angel's message. He was completely entrusting himself and his family to God's care. For God to direct him to Egypt, of all places, tapped into Old Testament history and prophecy in a further effort to help Israel recognize their King.

Before Israel was even a people, their forefathers were driven into Egypt, also out of dire necessity. First, their patriarch Joseph, then his father Jacob and all eleven of Joseph's brothers were placed by God in this foreign country for their safekeeping. Figuratively, as a nation, they were but a "child" as was Jesus. The passage quoted by Matthew, "Out of Egypt I called my son" (Hosea 11:1), originally referred to Israel, to their subsequent exodus from Egypt and return to Palestine. Matthew applied it to Jesus (v. 15) who was Israel's offspring and God's Son, to help them see that Jesus was theirs and they were His.

The depth of Herod's depravity is witnessed in his reaction to being fooled by the Magi and foiled from killing his royal rival (v. 16). God didn't cause his horrific behavior; Herod did, and it wasn't unusual behavior for him. In connection with the murder of three of his sons, he also killed at least three hundred of their attendants. He had large numbers of Jews executed on numerous occasions. At least once when he killed scores of perceived conspirators, he included all their family members in the annihilation.

In a village the size of Bethlehem and its vicinity, it's likely there were less than twenty boys aged two and younger. Though of little consequence to Herod, it would have been shattering to each family. Again, Matthew reaches into Old Testament Scripture to turn a word of history into a word of prophecy, this time echoing anguish rather than exodus (v. 17-18; Jeremiah 31:15).

When Jerusalem fell to Babylon in 586 BC, thus abolishing the nation, and when its residents were marched into exile hundreds of miles away, Ramah, a city five miles north of Jerusalem, was along their route.

Whatever the exact location of Rachel's burial site near Bethlehem (Genesis 35:19-20), it was a poignant image to depict this mother of Israel weeping from her grave for her departing children.

Before the families of Bethlehem would experience the joys of having a Savior, they would feel the utter sorrow caused by humanity's sinfulness.

Prayer: I celebrate the coming of the One who reaches into the utter depths of humanity's sin and sorrow with His salvation. Whether I experience or escape the awful intentions of others, I will ever keep my focus upon the certainty of salvation and will follow God's promptings in its direction.

Notes:

_____

_____

_____

_____

_____

_____

_____

_____

_____

_____

Personal Prayer:

_____

_____

_____

_____

_____

_____

_____

_____

_____

_____

_____

December 31

After Herod died, an angel of the Lord appeared in a dream to Joseph in Egypt and said, "Get up, take the child and his mother and go to the land of Israel, for those who were trying to take the child's life are dead." So he got up, took the child and his mother and went to the land of Israel. But when he heard that Archelaus was reigning in Judea in place of his father Herod, he was afraid to go there. Having been warned in a dream, he withdrew to the district of Galilee, and he went and lived in a town called Nazareth. So was fulfilled what was said through the prophets: "He will be called a Nazarene."

Matthew 2:19-23

The Plan Prevails

It's understandable to prefer that passages about King Herod not be included in any celebration of Christmas. The evil of this one man seems to have turned a sweet manger scene into extreme struggle and sadness.

In truth, nothing slipped out of God's control, not for a moment. The provision of Jesus had been securely in place "from the creation of the world" (Revelation 13:8). Across human history, including Israel's history, it may have seemed as if God's plan of redemption wasn't advancing. Events and outcomes appear to wander in all sorts of directions, but the plan would be brought to perfect completion, unswayable and unstoppable.

Herod's excessive evil couldn't begin to impede God's provision of a Savior. Even in his death, Herod planned to wield his diabolical power. Realizing people wouldn't mourn his passing, from his sickbed he ordered his sister to imprison prominent Jews inside an arena, ready for immediate execution when he died. This was his means of ensuring that sorrow would be associated with his death. Instead, his sister released the captives, adding to the people's rejoicing. Herod couldn't even control his sister, much less control God.

It's not known how long Joseph, Mary, and Jesus stayed in Egypt. There was a sizable settlement of Jews there, particularly in Alexandria, which was Egypt's second largest city. Joseph was told to remain until he received further instructions (v. 13). Sometime after

Herod's death, the instructions came (19). Through his third angelic visitation in a dream, Joseph was told to return to Israel (v. 20-21).

With Herod dead, his kingdom was divided between three of his sons. Judea, where Bethlehem and Jerusalem were located, was assigned to Archelaus (v. 22), the son who most followed in his father's footsteps. This region might have been Joseph and Mary's personal preference for a home. They would have known people in Bethlehem from their previous stay of approximately two years, the temple was in Jerusalem, and the area was away from questions about their marriage and the child's birth.

However, by means of a fourth dream, Joseph was warned to avoid Archelaus' reach (v. 22), a despot whose ruthlessness resulted in Rome deposing him within ten years. Instead, the family traveled to Galilee where Nazareth was located (v. 22-23). The district of Galilee had been assigned to another of Herod's sons, Herod Antipas. Though he was cruel enough to later order John the Baptist's beheading and mock Jesus upon His arrest, every detail of the Savior's coming was guarded by a divine plan that would navigate all obstacles.

There are indications in Matthew's wording (v. 23) that he's not quoting a specific Old Testament passage but merging multiple prophetic messages as to Jesus being "a Nazarene" or "of Nazareth." The words Nazareth and Nazarene come from the same word family as "branch," which is what the prophet Isaiah said would originate from the roots and stump of King David's father Jesse (Isaiah 11:1). Isaiah also spoke of the Coming One being despised (Isaiah 53:3), which is how people viewed anyone from the obscure town of Nazareth (John 1:46; 7:52).

God wasn't hindered by Jesus' coming being made difficult. The same Messiah would be from Bethlehem, from Egypt, and from Nazareth. This is because, in actuality, He is "from the creation of the world" (Revelation 13:8) and "for all the people" (Luke 2:10). When any plan is God's plan, it prevails no matter the challenges.

Prayer: I celebrate the coming of the One who is from the creation of the world and is for all the people. I lean into the certainty of His mission prevailing, not only across all of human history but also across my own life as I open my heart fully to His presence and purposes.

Notes:

___

___

___

___

___

___

___

___

___

Personal Prayer:

___

___

___

___

___

___

___

___

___

Made in the USA
Lexington, KY
17 November 2017